AF316828

Wait for the
Lightning

A fresh look at Genesis 1-12

Jeff Krogstad

Wait for the Lightning
A fresh look at Genesis 1-12

You can find Jeff at jeffkrogstad.com

ISBN: 979-8-218-34822-9 (paperback)
         979-8-218-35276-9 (hardcover)
         979-8-218-34823-6 (ebook)

Other Bible-focused books by Jeff Krogstad:

From Slavery to Freedom: *A personal reading of the Exodus Story*
New Wineskins: *A commentary on Luke's gospel*

Coming in 2024:

No Zombies? *A simple guide to the apocalypse and the book of Revelation*

*In the beginning,
God created the heavens
and the earth.*

Genesis 1:1

Table of Contents

Just so you know

I don't do systematic theology very well.

Systematic theology is where you create a more-or-less eternal statement about (to borrow a phrase from Doug Adams' *Hitchhiker's Guide to the Galaxy*) life, the universe, and everything. The nature of God. The condition of humanity. What, in fact, is reality?

A million years ago when I was in seminary we spent a great deal of time studying systematic theology. We dissected and analyzed reality to make it fit someone's system of thought. We categorized life into suffering, joy, vocation, sin, and lots of other columns that lie beautiful and lifeless like butterflies tacked to a board.

You can't categorize reality. You have to live it, and that's dangerous. When I wrote the first draft of this chapter, it was a rainy January day. Rain in January in Minnesota is a Very Bad Thing. The roads, the trees, the mailboxes, are all coated with ice. Cars shoot off into the snowbanks and find that the ice atop the snow is not thick enough to support them. Tow trucks skate and slither from there to here rescuing weary Saturday drivers standing by their stranded vehicles, coming down off a terrible adrenaline high. ("Why didn't I just stay home?") This is a metaphor for life. It's slippery and dangerous. Sooner or later you will end up in a ditch or you'll run into someone who is driving three miles an hour trying to be Very Careful.

What possible good would it do to try to systematize the experience? The result might read very much like a driver's training manual. "Under icy conditions, drivers must take extra caution to leave adequate stopping distance between vehicles. Reduce speeds and remain alert in order to avoid difficulties. If possible, travel should be delayed under such conditions. If you must drive, allow extra time. In the event that your vehicle begins to slide on the ice, steer into the slide in order to correct. Reduce speed and exercise extreme caution."

All good advice. But it bears zero resemblance to the actual experience of driving on ice: the adrenaline, white-knuckled, screaming-at-the-person-sitting-in-the-passenger's-seat-while-the-world-seems-to-rotate-three-hundred-and-sixty-degrees-around-you-at-fifty-miles-an-hour-just-before-you-call-the-towtruck experience. The systematized version bears as much similarity to the experience as a carefully pinned dead butterfly on cardboard bears to a gypsy moth swooping through the dark in search of a candle.

Like the driver's ed manual, we try to categorize and quantify and understand God. We attempt to pour the wide ocean of God into the tiny little hole in the sand of our brains. If you want to understand the ocean, don't try to analyze it. Take a kayak out beyond the breakers and you'll know the ocean in a whole new way. If you want to understand a thunderstorm, don't read about low pressure systems and cumulonimbus clouds. Instead, when that purple wall cloud comes rushing in from the southwest, climb an oak tree and hang on for dear life while you wait for the lightning. Listen to the branches creak and groan. Feel the lightning smack and pop into the forest around you. Wonder if the sheets of cold rain coming down will extinguish the flames. (This is also a great way to learn about prayer, by the way.) If you want to know about love, don't start with a book. Go get your heart tangled up in a relationship with someone who really matters to you.

Genesis isn't giving us a systematic picture of all the truth about God in a nicely categorized passage. We do a lot of damage when we try to make the Bible into systematic theology. The creation story in Genesis is like a chaperone at the beginning of a dance introducing us to our new partner. "Jeff, this is the universe. Universe, meet Jeff." I hold out my hands cautiously. I think we're going to do the waltz I stumbled through in fifth grade phy ed. The Universe grabs me with an iron grip and whirls off into a tarantella. All the while God is grinning and playing his fiddle and singing faster and faster. (Look closely at Michelangelo's painting of God on the ceiling of the Sistine Chapel and you can see an uncanny resemblance to Charlie Daniels. Accident? I don't think so.) At this point I have a choice. I can say, "Sorry, broke a heel, thanks anyway, thirsty, need to get some punch." I can go sit along the edge of the gym in the dark. Most of us sit over there, watching the dancers and complaining about the band.

Or I can fumble and flop and try to keep up and laugh and get my foot stepped on and sweat and enjoy every second of it.

It's only fair to tell you that dancing terrifies me and I'm horrible at it.

Theology, the study of the things of God, is about context. It's about living in love with God where you are, in this particular slice of life, to the deepest and fullest extent possible. As we're working through Genesis, you might think I've missed something important. Go back and focus on it and figure out why that piece is stuck in your throat. What is God saying? That's your context. I'll be over on the other side of the forest, climbing as high as I can, hanging on for dear life, waiting for the lightning and laughing my heart out.

Why study Genesis?

There are several good reasons. For one, it's a foundational text that has shaped our culture and our world. These words written in ancient Hebrew carry a strength and power that weaves through our own art and literature like no other text.

Genesis lays the foundations not only for art and culture, but for knowing God. These words set the foundation for knowing God as Creator, obviously, but also as Redeemer.

These few chapters set up the issues which shape the rest of the Bible. Not only do these chapters set the stage for the biblical texts, but also for the 2000-year sweep of biblical history. For those who are willing to accept these texts as God-given foundations, they explain our own history. They shed light on the grand movements of world history as well as our own intimate, personal histories.

The rest of the Bible takes these chapters very seriously. Jesus referred to them multiple times and obviously considered them foundational.

Those are just a few reasons for studying Genesis.

There is plenty of conflict in our day about the idea of God creating the world. Most people who care about the creation-evolution debate have isolated themselves into a particular camp, and there's very little dialogue about Genesis anymore. It's interesting that the people who seem most engaged with these stories in the last few decades are the psychologists. They dig into these texts to explain who we are and why we do what we do. Jordan Peterson, for example, is a Canadian psychologist who draws massive crowds and a huge online following as he discusses biblical texts from a psychological perspective.

Digging into Genesis comes with a few challenges. We need to recognize that we are a secondary audience. God speaks through the Bible to each person who will hear. So you can hear his voice in these texts. But when we come to study these chapters, we need to know that we're not the initial audience. You probably don't speak or write in ancient Hebrew. Our culture and approach to reality is very different than those ancient people who were the first audience of these texts.

The Hebrews were also surrounded by many diverse cultures. Each people group had their own religions and their own gods. Some of them had their own scriptures. The ancient Babylonians, for example, had the Enuma Elish. They believed in a creation story that revolved around Tiamat and Apsu. They read the Epic of Gilgamesh.

The Babylonians are just one example. The Canaanites, Hittites, Egyptians, and many others impacted the ancient Hebrews during the centuries when these scriptures were being written down. That shapes these words in significant ways.

We live in a much different context, making assumptions that would be foreign to the ancient Hebrews. We typically come to these Genesis texts asking When and How. Those are the two questions that have generated so much conflict in our world. When did the universe come into being? How did it happen? We tend to define truth in a very narrow way. We pit scientific truth against spiritual truth and see them as separate things.

The ancient Hebrews asked questions that might never occur to us. They asked Who and What and Why. They asked, what does this mean for us today? Unlike us, they saw the spiritual and physical worlds as intimately intertwined. Genesis is designed to carefully answer these questions. If we are willing to suspend our own questions, we might find ourselves learning a lot from the ancients.

There are some good reasons to ask when and how the universe was created. Various ways of answering those questions generate a lot of heat around the Bible. I won't address those questions much in this book. I don't want to spend my time looking in the rearview mirror and arguing about the past.

Those ancient Hebrews focused on the present, though they looked to the past to answer questions about the present. Learning from their example, we'll ask questions like these:

- Who is God? What is he up to?
- Who are we? What is our situation?
- Why do we do the things we do?
- What does God want for us?

My goal in this book is to approach Genesis in this kind of a Hebrew way. I don't worry much, honestly, about what happened fifteen billion years ago or in 4004 BC or whenever. It's not that I'm unconcerned with history. I'm an avid student of history, especially biblical history. But in this context, I want to approach Genesis in the way that Hebrew thinkers might approach it. I want to comprehend what's going on in our lives today.

So fair warning: I will consistently sidestep the questions of the Big Bang, how old the earth is, whether "yom" in the Hebrew of Genesis 1 denotes a twenty-four hour day, etc. I'm not even going to speculate about the dinosaurs and where they fit into the timeline. I won't deal with it. That's really going to frustrate some of you in a book about Genesis. Maybe it frustrates you because you approach this book as if it is about what happened back then. I'm approaching it as if it will tell me who we are in the present, why we do what we do, and most importantly, who God is.

I can hear you thinking: Yes, but if Genesis isn't *true*, then the rest of the Bible isn't trustworthy either.

Let's get this one out of the way right off the bat: Genesis is true. It is God's word, holy and without fault. Like the rest of the Bible, it is true. If you let it, Genesis will read you. That's what the Bible does, as the writer says in Hebrews 4:12. "For the word of God is alive and powerful. It is sharper than the sharpest two-edged sword, cutting between soul and spirit, between joint and marrow. It exposes our innermost thoughts and desires." Scripture reads us.

That's the way I'm going to interact with Genesis, because it's God's word. Historical truth is only one kind of truth, and not the most important kind. We too often confuse something being factual with it being true. The most important truths go far, far beyond being simply factual. (If this is your issue and you really want to dive in, see the Appendix on biblical authority at the end of the book.)

If you want to focus on what happened in the past, that's your option. Maybe you've argued so much about what happened back then that you can't even get out of that box when you're dealing with Genesis. If you think narrow post-Enlightenment definitions of "truth" can somehow put God in handcuffs and make him play by your rules, you've got a lot more brass than I do. He was the one that caused the text to be written in this way, after all.

Here's my suggestion, if you want to think about the past: Go read a book about something else. I don't want to frustrate you. Pick up one of the gospels and read that. All your concerns about historicity are totally legitimate in the gospels. Have fun.

Still reading? Okay. Here we go.

Starting at the Beginning: Genesis 1:1

In college I took a World Literature class. We studied all kinds of ancient writings including several passages from the Bible, notably selections from Genesis and Isaiah. Our discussion on Genesis still hangs vivid in my mind. Our class of a dozen or so students spent 45 minutes chewing on the words, "In the beginning."

What did it mean? Why not give a date? Why jump in like that? When is the beginning? Is there anything before the beginning? *Could* there be anything before the beginning? How does or doesn't this mesh with scientific understandings of the Big Bang? What about the primordial formation of galaxies, solar systems, planets and all the rest? What is the agenda of the writer here? Why choose this phrase? Who is the audience?

Think about that word, *beginning.* There's a lot implied in that one word. Some of the cultures surrounding the Hebrews believed that time moved in great eternal cycles. Every so many years the great cycles would repeat. In contrast, Genesis says time has a beginning. Time is linear. It is finite. It has a beginning, and by implication, it will also have an end. The idea of time coming to an end is an important theme in the Bible.

My head spun as we discussed all these things. We spent the rest of the class, another 45 minutes, on the word "God." An hour and a half on four words. I walked out of class totally amazed at the candor and depth of this discussion at a secular university. We talked in depth about the nature of God as we understood it. Various people in the class shared their assumptions about what they think when they hear the word "God." We contrasted the personal God of the Hebrews with the non-theism of the Buddhists, the multiplicity of gods in Hinduism, and the impersonal God of deism. It was a stunning discussion.

I find it fascinating that the Bible makes no argument for the existence of God. Here he is. Boom! *In the beginning, God.*

Thomas Aquinas was a brilliant thinker who lived in the 1200's AD. At that time, the work of Aristotle (which had been lost to western cultures for centuries) was re-introduced into Latin. Aristotle became accessible to western Europe for the first time in a thousand years. Aquinas did an amazing intellectual job of taking Aristotle's thought and integrating it into Christian frameworks. As part of this work, Aquinas came up with several "proofs" for the existence of God. For example: Everything has a cause, said Aquinas. That cause has been caused by something else, and if you trace that back far enough you come to an uncaused Cause. That First Cause must be God.

I've never found Aquinas' proofs very helpful. I like what the Bible does. "In the beginning, God…" No arguments, no proofs, no logic, just presence. A story, if you like.

It almost sounds like "Once upon a time," doesn't it?

God seems quite content to let the Bible tell this story about him without appealing to logic or proofs. *In the beginning God.* Here he is. If his presence makes you uncomfortable, it's simply a story, so you can blow it off.

You might be really uncomfortable with this word, "story." Yet God seems okay with it. Maybe that's because he knows the story hangs in the back of our minds and the back of our hearts and doesn't let us escape. Stories have power like that. Ever tried to forget an off-color joke? It keeps coming to mind because stories are powerful. This story of God keeps haunting us.

I think the best way to read the Bible is to show up as if it was an enormous negotiation. Kind of like a job interview for a position that really matters to you. Imagine walking into a conference room knowing that the next few minutes will define the rest of your life. Imagine yourself carrying a briefcase that holds your sense of who you are, your beliefs, your hopes and dreams. You open your briefcase and spread out your key documents in front of you, and you prepare to negotiate. The interviewer has some ideas and expectations about the position and whether what you bring has value. In turn, you have a sense of who you are and what you might bring that is important. Together, can the two of you come to an agreement?

When we open the Bible, are we prepared to engage in this way? Are we prepared to encounter all God wants for us? Are we willing to face God in this way, recognizing all that is at stake?

Most of us read the Bible as if it is samples day at the grocery store. We sample a little bit of this, taste a little bit of that. We like the cheddar cheese spread and crackers, so we buy that product. But the pizza bites have a weird flavor. No thank you. We sample the Bible here and there, avoiding the disturbing or confusing parts.

Maybe we should come at it like negotiating a new job. Or a new life. We may find that some of what we bring to the table is totally useless and needs to be discarded. But we may find that other things we bring are surprisingly valuable. They reflect the very image of the God we meet in these stories. We begin to realize that these things are of supreme value. The Bible will redefine us. Reading the Bible can and should be a life-defining exercise.

It's worth mentioning here that the word translated "God" in this part of the Bible isn't so much a name as it is a title. In Hebrew it's something like "Elohim." It is kind of a generic word for "God" or "gods" either in reference to the God of the Hebrews or those of other cultures. Later in the Bible other words and names for God show up.

That's one reason why it's so significant when God shares his name with Moses in Exodus 3.

Most Bibles have an introduction that seldom gets read. In it the translators explain (among other things) how they translate each of the Hebrew names for God into English, and how you can know as you read which Hebrew terms are being used.

It's not important for a beginning reader to distinguish these things. Whether the Hebrew writer uses the term Elohim or YHWH or Adonai or something else, it's the same Person that's being talked about.

God shows up here in the beginning. Throughout the Bible, God keeps doing this same thing. He'll show up, every time.

We need to engage him in the same way. We need to come to the table. We need to show up ready to negotiate. Come ready to deal as if your life depends on it. According to the rest of the Bible, that's exactly what is at stake.

The important thing is to be in the conversation. Bring your questions and certainties and all. Read the stories. Chew on the mysteries. Wrestle with the questions. Laugh at the jokes. It's not the fastest way to read the Bible, but this isn't a contest.

Creator: Genesis 1:1

In the beginning God created. It's part of what God does.

A cabinetmaker designs a china cabinet to custom-fit a space in his mother's house. A farmer manufactures a part to coax a few more years of life out of an old plow. The consummate hostess plans a party. The chef crafts a culinary masterpiece. Painters and musicians, writers and mechanics, city planners and teachers and architects and plumbers all reflect the image of God by creating stuff.

What is this act of creating?

Five hundred years ago, a stubborn German monk named Martin Luther wrote this about God's creativity:

> I believe that God has made me and all
> creatures; that He has given me my body and
> soul, eyes, ears, and all my limbs, my reason,
> and all my senses, and still preserves them; in
> addition thereto, clothing and shoes, meat and
> drink, house and homestead, wife and children,
> fields, cattle, and all my goods; that He
> provides me richly and daily with all that I need
> to support this body and life, protects me from
> all danger, and guards me and preserves me
> from all evil; and all this out of pure, fatherly,
> divine goodness and mercy, without any merit
> or worthiness in me; for all which I owe it to
> Him to thank, praise, serve, and obey Him.
> This is most certainly true.

Creation is a diverse and complex business. It involves everything from aardvarks to zebras, from shoes to family, the spending money in your pocket and the Himalayas. Seeing God as creator is a view we will never fully grasp, for we can never fully grasp creation itself.

God stands over and outside his creation as the Creator. To complicate matters, God is not only outside creation, but is also present in it. And present *to* it in some sense. So not only is God the cosmic watch-maker who set things spinning once upon a time; God is also moving through his creation and constantly changing and updating it. And God is present in it in a way that created things can contact him and relate to him.

When we think of God as Creator we are often tempted to envision him in a static pose much like Michelangelo's God on the ceiling of the Sistine Chapel, reaching out his finger to touch Adam and bring him to life. But I like Tony Campolo's picture of God as creator. He asks, have you ever watched a little child playing a game? Swing them in the air and they giggle and as soon as their feet touch the ground they say, "Do it again!" Campolo pictures God making something simple, trivial, like a daisy. Out of his thought, his hands, his words springs a flower. He's so excited he giggles and says, "Do it again! Do it again! Do it again!" Pretty soon there's a whole field of daisies. Think how many times you have to rinse and repeat this idea to get just Minnesota, let alone the universe.

We can't leave this word "created" without touching two key ideas:

First, God created you. He is absolutely madly crazy in love, passionate about you, because you are his creation. Because God created you, he loves you. He protects you. He delights in your achievements and grieves for your losses. It is the overflowing of God's limitless love that resulted in your creation. You look in the mirror and see a worn leather bag of sin, fault, trouble, wrinkles, failures, disappointments, and tragedy. God looks in your face and sees the pinnacle of his creation.

I am not making this up. This is the tip of the iceberg of what it means when we say that God loves you. Just the tip.

Second, (jumping ahead a little bit) God made you in his image. We'll have a lot more to say about that later. But for now suffice it to say that you are creative because God has made you creative, as a reflection of how he himself is creative. There are activities that bring you deep joy because God wove those into your being. Yes, there has been some trouble along the way, and yes, there are some things you do that aren't what God wants. Don't focus on those things for the moment. Right now, we need to see that we are created, you and me, to do certain things that bring joy to us. God wired that desire and that appetite for joy into our beings.

Maybe it's teaching. Maybe it's rebuilding an engine or talking with a lonely person or baking pumpkin bread. Knowing God as creator means that you acknowledge his Godhood by doing what he created you to do. Coyotes are created to hunt. Trout are created to swim. What are you created to do? What activities bring deep, deep joy to your heart? This doesn't mean you have to make your living at these activities. (Why must we make this so complicated?) It just means you find a way to do the stuff that's in your heart.

God delights in creating. He is passionate about his creation, like the cabinetmaker or the chef or the teacher. He created you to be passionate about some part of his creation as well, and to live in his image. Following that design will bring you joy and will benefit the rest of creation.

Who did God create you to be?

Visions of Heaven?

When I was a little kid in third grade, my Sunday School teacher gave us an assignment. We were assigned the task of drawing a picture of what we thought heaven looked like. I drew a giant triangular something-or-other with a cross on it and a doorway underneath, clouds all around. I scrounged a yellow crayon to somehow include my impression that the light from the throne of God was leaking out. Even at the time the picture underwhelmed me.

I think that's what we so often do with this idea of heaven. We make it about a place, a nice place, a place we all want to go because it's so nice. We imagine it to be like Minnesota but without winter or mosquitoes or road construction. And the Scandinavians will all be happy.

Weird.

But the Bible doesn't say that God created heaven. It says he created "the heavens and the earth." Then the text goes on in great detail about the earth, but we don't talk much about the heavens. A little bit with creating stars and birds and other things that fly above our heads. We don't get much detail, only a wistful sense that there's something good (heavenly, even) that is out of our reach.

In ancient Hebrew culture, or in any culture prior to the Wright Brothers or Sputnik, it was easy to imagine God up there somewhere. We made heaven, the place where God lived, synonymous with "the heavens" by which we meant whatever is above the sky.

Is that what the Bible is talking about? The Bible doesn't seem interested in revealing some otherworldly place where God has set up shop. Rather, it seems bent on helping us understand that God is present here. We just fail to see.

Read Isaiah 6:1-9, for example. Talk about a picture of God being present here and now. Isaiah sees a vision of God. He starts by saying, "I saw the Lord. He was sitting on a lofty throne…" and goes on from there. Isaiah doesn't see this vision up above the sky someplace. Instead, he's standing in the temple in Jerusalem when he sees God.

In the Bible, God is constantly coming to meet people on solid ground, in the stuff of everyday life. Abraham meets God while he's resting in the shade on a hot day. Ezekiel meets God on a riverbank. After Jesus rises from the dead, his followers meet God where they're hiding in an upper room in a house in Jerusalem. In the book of Acts, Paul meets God while he's traveling to the city of Damascus.

What if "the heavens" is referring not to some separate abode of God, such that God has to leave home to come to earth? What if "the heavens" is referring to a spiritual realm that exists alongside us? What if God is all around us but hidden from our perception? "The heavens" is the dwelling place of God. It is not separate from the physical creation, but simply hidden alongside it.

I know we have a lot of songs that talk about Jesus leaving heaven to come to earth. It's a common theme in Christian teaching.

That's a simplified understanding of heaven, but it isn't necessarily biblical. The Bible verses that are often quoted to support this idea are 2 Corinthians 8:9 and Philippians 2:7.

Neither of those verses says that Jesus left heaven. 2 Corinthians says that though Jesus was rich, he became poor for your sake. Philippians says that Christ emptied himself, taking the form of a slave.

If you do a Bible search and look at the term "heavens," you'll find initially that in most places early on in the Bible, it sounds like "heavens" is just another word for sky. The Bible refers many times to the "birds of the heavens," for example. That doesn't seem to mean some strange kind of spiritual birds. The New Living Translation gets the sense of the Hebrew when it says, "Let the skies be filled with birds of every kind."

Later on, starting with Ezekiel and some of the other later prophets, and especially in the New Testament, you begin to hear about God "opening the heavens" to reveal spiritual things to his people.

When Jesus is baptized, the Bible says that the heavens were opened. What happens next isn't a vision of what's above the sky. Rather God shows up in the form of a dove and a voice, speaking to Jesus and those around about his identity.

This shift, from heaven being an above-the-sky-house-for-God to the heavens being a parallel dimension alongside our own physical reality, would make sense of a lot of the Bible. When Ephesians 2:6 says that we are seated with Christ "in the heavenly realms" it doesn't mean that we have a chair reserved in that great picnic shelter in the sky. Rather it seems to mean that the spiritual reality of our lives has changed. The presence of God in Jesus changes us. These changes are at least partly hidden from us. But they are potent and important nonetheless.

God is not limited to some spiritual world, but he created that as well. He created both the spiritual and the physical. He is not limited by his nature as a spiritual being any more than he is limited by Jesus taking on physical flesh.

According to the Bible, God is present in this creation. In the same way you can see that creation is broken, God can see it. He is aware of the pain and the decay. Because he loves this broken world and all that is in it so much, he has plans to make it right. And especially if you take 2 Peter seriously, when God decides to redo all of creation, it will mean a total recreation of not only the physical world but the spiritual realms as well.

Peter describes a "new heavens and a new earth." And John picks up on the same theme in the last book of the Bible, Revelation. The final culmination of John's vision is this new creation. What John describes is a beautiful city that comes down out of the heavens. Then John says that God's home is now among his people..

God longs to live with his creation. He longs to bring heaven and earth together into one.

From the image of God walking in the garden of Eden in the cool of the day in Genesis 3 to God dwelling with humanity in Revelation, this is the major focus of the Bible. The central focus of the Bible is Jesus, God in human form, living among us. At his birth in Matthew's gospel Jesus is called "Emmanuel," which means "God with us."

Jesus brings heaven to earth. He taught us to pray that God's will would be done and his kingdom would come on earth as it is in the heavens.

Another shift that happens when we start to read "the heavens" in this way. Jesus talked a lot about "the kingdom of heaven." Many Christians assume he's talking about going to heaven when we die. But a careful reading of Jesus' words shows that is not what he's talking about. He seems to be describing that spiritual realm that exists just out of our reach. He started so many of his parables by saying, "The kingdom of heaven is like…" He wants us to understand God and his ways.

Maybe Jesus wasn't so much about herding us into heaven after we die. Maybe he was trying to tell us that God's ways are accessible to us here and now.

Eventually heaven will be great. I'm looking forward to it. But the Bible seems much more interested in God getting his heavenly way in this life first.

Hidden agendas

There is something going on in Genesis 1 that we usually miss. The cultures around the ancient Hebrews had a variety of gods. Each of these gods was responsible for a specific area of life. For example, the Egyptian god Huh (or Heh) was responsible for time. When you see him depicted in the stone carvings in Egypt, he's holding a reed in each hand. Apparently each of these reeds represented a million years to the Egyptians.

But Genesis 1 says that God started at the beginning. God was already Lord of time. God was already master of the area Huh claimed as his responsibility. Later in the chapter God will create the separation of day from night. He will create stars that serve as markers for days and seasons and years. He's marking out time, taking charge of Huh's domain.

Do you see how the text, very subtly, is saying that God is sovereign over Huh?

This is happening over and over again in the text. Baal, the god of the Canaanites, was god of lush vegetation. God created all the growing plants. He is sovereign over Baal.

The Babylonians believed that Apsu created the earth from the body of Tiamat, his wife. He was the god of fresh water. She was the goddess of chaos and the sea. When Genesis says that God's Spirit was hovering over the chaotic waters and then God began to create, do you hear the claim? God tells the water where to go, and it goes. God is sovereign over Tiamat and Apsu.

The Egyptians worshiped Thoth, the god of the moon. Horus was their god of birds and the sky and good order. Both of their domains are created by God in Genesis 1.

Marduk was the patron god of Babylon. When the Babylonians looked up in the night sky and saw Jupiter, they believed they were seeing Marduk. Genesis said that God created the planets and the stars. God is sovereign over Marduk.

We miss all of this because we are not Hebrews living in the ancient world, surrounded by the gods of other cultures. We miss the symbolism and the claims the text is making.

That's why it is important to dig beyond the surface. It's important to go beyond our own assumptions and questions. We didn't even know we should be wondering about Marduk. But the Bible thinks it's important to tell us that God is sovereign over him.

What gods are competing for your loyalty? Who else is claiming your allegiance? How is God telling you he's a higher priority than those other gods?

Another fact hides under this text. In most of the ancient world, especially in Babylon, the origin stories told about the gods creating this world almost by accident. Humans were most often created by the gods to function as slaves when things needed doing. Genesis lays out a whole different understanding of God's purposes in creating humans. We'll dig into that a lot more when we get near the end of Genesis 1.

Chaos: Genesis 1:1-3

To repeat: We think differently than the ancient Hebrews. Our minds have been trained to value a certain kind of logic, to see things in columns of true vs. false and to separate things into neat categories (spiritual vs. material, for example). A long line of human history has trained us *not* to understand what the Bible has to say.

This gets a little deep into the weeds. But it's important. Your brain and mine, because of the way we have grown up and how we've been trained to think, are far removed from the original readers of the Bible. For example, one of the most important events that has shaped our thinking here in the 21st century is what is sometimes called "the Enlightenment." That period of history in the 1700's (and echoing into the 1800's and beyond) shaped how we think today. Rational thought and scientific observation became cornerstones of human intelligence.

It's not that people couldn't reason before that, of course. But the Enlightenment thinkers taught us to believe that if you can't measure something, it doesn't exist. Or at least it exists less importantly, somehow. Have you ever watched those crazy shows where people go investigate haunted houses? They always have some guy with his invented gadget that can pick up weird spiritual energies. We are constantly trying to measure things.

It's not only about what you can measure, but about what you do with what you can measure. Human reason is more important than anything else, according to the Enlightenment. This kind of thinking has given us some amazing gifts. For example, I've been a type-1 diabetic since I was seven years old. I am alive today because scientists figured out how insulin functions in the human body, and how to create it (there's that creativity again) and put it into sterile bottles so it can be injected into my body and keep me alive. I wear an insulin pump that does an incredible job of working with a continuous glucose monitor to give me tiny little doses of insulin throughout the day so I don't have to take injections all the time. All that is possible because of Enlightenment thinking and the scientific advances that followed it.

I'm a fan.

But we also have to recognize that this idea, this belief that human reason is above all and if something isn't measurable it's not "real," this idea that gives us so many good gifts also takes something away from us. Something important.

It's hard for the post-Enlightenment mind to grasp things like good and evil. The existence of evil is a mystery that the post-Enlightenment mind doesn't want to accept. Love and hate are the same way, because emotions don't seem rational. We reduce love and hate to fickle emotions, far less trustworthy than facts. Mythology is reduced to a bunch of cute stories. Faith becomes a crutch that's fine if you need that sort of thing. Worship is weird and doesn't make sense to our brains. None of the things I've listed in this paragraph are measurable. And yet, what would life be without them?

To the Hebrew mind, chaos is very closely related to evil. So when Genesis says that "the earth was formless and empty" it's a statement about chaos. There's no order, no system, no function, no good. It's chaos, and the result of chaos is that the earth is void. It's empty in the sense of its value. It has no usefulness. It has no connection to the purposes of God.

Ever feel like your life is formless and empty? So many of us do. Think how much structure is imposed on your life. Think about how your life is regulated by the kinds of structure that would be foreign to the ancient Hebrews. How many clocks can you see right now? How many appointments are on your calendar for the next week? What schedules—school, work, television, trains, flights, appointments, whatever—do you hold in your head? What structures have you memorized if you start to think about road maps, store maps, mall maps, airport maps, website maps? We are structured down to our toenails. Yet (and this is partly because of the structure) our lives so often feel formless and empty. So often we feel totally chaotic.

The creation account is largely about God imposing good order onto chaos. So many of us have taken the good gift of God to the nth degree and created a whole new kind of chaos. We have over-structured and over-scheduled our lives to the point where the form has become void, the structure has become chaotic. In our desperate need for control, we structure ourselves to death.

The earth was formless and empty, and darkness covered the deep waters. Is it dark over the deep places in your heart? Is there an impenetrable veil over the canyons of your heart?

One of the truths the Bible tells us that is sometimes hard to hear is that the depths of our hearts often betray us. We are prone to hide things away there. We hide old hurts, fears, bitterness, abandoned hopes. All these get piled up in the depths of our hearts but they do not go away. We find ourselves acting and speaking in ways that mystify us because we do not realize that "what you say flows from what is in your heart" (Luke 6:45). The things hidden in the depths still move and manipulate us.

The word of God reveals a whole new level of chaos in our lives when it points our attention toward the depths of our hearts.

But the story doesn't stop there. That is the "before" picture. The next line is critical, and (as often happens in the Bible) there are some word plays going on here. The Bible is mostly written in two ancient languages, Hebrew and Greek. You don't need to get a degree in ancient languages to understand the Bible. But every once in a while a little information about ancient words can help us.

In both Hebrew and Greek, the words for "wind" and "spirit" and "breath" are identical. In Hebrew, the language in which Genesis was originally written, this word is pronounced something like *ruach*. Some translations say that a wind from God was blowing over the waters. Others say the Spirit of God was hovering over the waters. Both are accurate to the Hebrew. Both translations are legitimate, and neither is complete. I like the term one translation uses, that the Spirit of God was "brooding" over the chaos.

God comprehends the depths. He knows the formless void. But chaos is unable to comprehend God. The nature of chaos leaves it alienated from God, unable to reach out. But God hovers, broods, plots for good in the midst of chaos.

Is it helpful to know that in those chaotic places in your life, God's Spirit is brooding, hovering, flowing, breathing? That the hidden depths of your heart are hidden to you, but not to God? God will speak and bring light into that darkness. But we're getting ahead of ourselves.

For the moment, look at the world around you. What examples of chaos, emptiness, darkness do you see? What evidences do you see that the Spirit of God is moving?

Light: Genesis 1:1-5

God speaks. Two words in Hebrew. "Let there be light" in English. The immediate result is "and there was light." God's word is powerful and has immediate results.

Anticipating the turn of the millennium as the year 2000 approached, Life magazine made a list of the hundred most influential people in the last thousand years. When you think back over the last thousand years of history, lots of names come to the fore: scientists, explorers, statesmen, even a theologian or two. Who would you choose for number one on a list like that?

Life magazine chose Thomas Edison. His invention of the light bulb has totally revolutionized how we live. If you want to do an amazing experiment, try doing without artificial light for 24 hours. No inside lights, no flashlights, no headlights, no LED lights, no illuminated clocks or watches or computer screens. I spend lots of time in wilderness situations. I love backcountry canoeing, hunting, and camping. And I don't think I have ever gone without artificial light for 24 hours. It's an intriguing idea.

Think of the difference light makes in your life. Think how dependent most of us are on our eyes. Some of the people I've learned the most from are those who live without physical sight. They learn to rely on other ways of gaining information, other ways of navigating, other ways of "seeing". They have a lot to teach.

When God starts creating, he begins with light. Whether you imagine this first moment of creation as a brilliant Big Bang 14 billion years ago, or as a sudden appearance of light emanating from God's being six thousand years ago, doesn't matter a great deal. God begins the creation by creating light.

1 John 1 helps us understand part of why this might be. John tells us, "God is light and there is no darkness in him at all." What might this mean on a literal level? What might it mean metaphorically? Think of all the associations we have in our language with light. Look at this list and think through what it might mean to use each of these words or expressions, especially if we use them to refer to people:

Brilliant
In the dark
Dim
Bright
Enlightened
Dark
Illuminating
Luminous

Can you think of others that belong on the list? In our language and in our thinking, light is almost always a positive thing. We treasure brightness and color, both attributes of light.

Think what light makes possible. From a biological point of view, there would be no life without light. Photosynthesis in plants becomes one of the key building blocks for all life. Your skin absorbs sunlight and miraculously manufactures vitamin D. Sensors in your brain release chemicals in response to light that make you feel happy and well balanced. The lack of these chemicals sends some people into seasonal depression. A few years ago I turned down a job offer on beautiful Resurrection Bay in Seward, Alaska. I had lived seven years in Seattle with 50 inches of rain each year, and I wasn't bothered by that. Much. But I couldn't imagine living in a place that gets three times that much rain. I needed light, and the gray clouds of Seward intimidated me.

The very act of reading could not happen without light. The deeper you dig, the greater you realize is your dependence on light. Most of us have never thought about this. It is staggering.

So if God is light and in him there is no darkness, such that your reading lamp, my laptop screen, the hundred watt bulbs in my garage, and even the sun are just dim reflections of his glory, what does that say about your utter, largely unrealized, dependence on him?

And there was light: Genesis 1:3

And there was light. Seems so matter-of-fact, doesn't it? God said it, and it happened.

Two questions.

First, what would happen in your life if you had this ability to make your words into reality?

Second, what would happen in your life if you truly believed this about God?

First topic. Our words have power. When we speak, things change. Maybe it's not so obvious as "let there be light, and there was light," but what about other words? What about these:

"I'm proud of you."
"You are beautiful."
"I love you."
"I hate you."
"You are a failure."

Do these words have power? Better believe it. When you speak, things change.

We see this most clearly with the hurtful words. Even if you don't mean those words, they change things. Even if you're simply speaking out of the woundedness of your heart, those words change things, create wounds in other hearts. A friend of mine says, "Hurt people hurt people." Our words carry that hurt and inflict it on others. Jesus said once that it is out of the overflow of our own hearts that our mouths speak. So when our hearts are full of wounds and damage, we speak wounds and damage into others.

But it's also true of the words that build people up. Have you ever known someone whose words were consistently positive, upbuilding, helpful, loving? As long as there is sincerity behind those positive words, you want to be with that person. You want to spend more time with them, because it's a healing thing, a life-giving thing.

So maybe we do have this ability, more than we know. Our words change things. The Bible says it a little differently. "You will always harvest what you plant" (see Galatians 6:7). When we plant bitter, hurtful words, we will reap a terrible harvest sooner or later. When we plant deceit, arrogance, duplicity, the harvest is coming. Similarly, when we plant truth, compassion, gentleness, integrity, the harvest is coming. Count on it. It starts with our words.

But what about God's words? This brings us to the second topic. What would happen if we really believed that God was as good as his word? So look at some of the words God speaks in scripture. Do we believe these words?

"Do not be afraid."
"Do not be afraid, for I have ransomed you; I have called you by name."
"You are mine."
"I know the plans I have for you, plans for good and not for disaster."
"When you go through the deep waters, I will be with you."
"Here on earth you will have many trials and sorrows. But take heart, because I have overcome the world."
"I am going to prepare a place for you."
"I no longer call you slaves, but friends."

What would it mean to believe, down at the core of our being, that these words are true, and directed to us? What would change today if you knew that God called you his friend? If you knew beyond any doubt that God has good plans for you?

This business of speaking is powerful. God says, "Let there be light" and the light appears. We say, "I love you" and the words call forth love in response. God speaks to us and says, "Do not be afraid." Are we willing to listen and let the words shape us and call forth a God-given confidence in the face of trouble?

One of Jesus' followers wrote about this in a letter, roughly twenty-five years after Jesus rose from the dead. He wrote that God, who said, "Let there be light in the darkness," has made this light shine in our hearts so we could know the glory of God that is seen in the face of Jesus Christ. (See 2 Corinthians 4.) In other words, part of what the Bible is saying about this is that God is still speaking, saying "let there be light" where there is darkness in your life. He is calling light into your heart, letting his glory shine into you and through you.

That's good news. There is so much darkness around us. And there is so much darkness in us. But God continues to speak light into us. It is true that we speak out of the overflow of our hearts, and this is true of God as well. God's heart for you, and for this dark world, is love. Out of the fullness of his love he speaks light and life into us.

And it was good: Genesis 1:3-5

Here's an important question that might seem at first like just so much philosophical trivia:

Is something "Good" because God says it's good, or is there a greater idea of "good" that God is bound to follow? Another way to ask the same question: Does "good" reflect some moral abstraction, or does it reflect the personality of God?

I believe God determines what is good based on his own nature. So if something (beauty, kindness, intimacy, health, courage) lines up with God's character, it is good. Our definitions of words like these matter. We might use those same words to describe things that appeal to us, but are the opposite of God's heart. In that case our notion of beauty or of courage is a twisted mistake.

Why is this important?

Because, simply, if we can know "good" apart from knowing God, we have the authority to make up our own minds. We get to decide what is positive. We never have to submit our wills to God.

Jumping ahead a couple chapters, this is precisely the sin of the garden of Eden. This refusal to submit to God is often the reason why people and organizations get derailed and turn in on themselves to pursue their own agendas. Well meaning people who decide they know what is "good" and pursue it apart from the primary agenda of knowing, loving, and submitting to God, tend to end up in a swamp.

Eve and Adam chose to eat the fruit in the garden in order to know how to discern Good from Evil apart from God. (Much more about that later.) But here in Genesis 1, God himself declares what is "good." Making up our own minds is an ongoing temptation for us.

Into the weeds for a moment: Dietrich Bonhoeffer was a Christian pastor who was executed by Hitler's order days before Germany surrendered in 1945. In his final book, *Ethics* (which he never completed but which was assembled and published after his death), he says something about this. Bonhoeffer states that deciding what is good for ourselves means we are missing the mark. He says that we are created to know only one thing, and that is God. We are created to know all other things through God. When we try to make up our minds apart from God, we are in rebellion just like Adam and Eve. Taking this into the later parts of the Bible, we might say that it is only by knowing Jesus can we truly know what God considers good. This is because it is in Jesus that God reveals his heart and his plan for us.

To put it another way, a thing is good inasmuch as it resembles and reflects Jesus. If it is unlike Jesus, it is not good.

Yet over and over again we are tempted to make up our own minds about right and wrong, good and bad, without ever seeking Jesus or his guidance on these questions. We decide a thing is good and we pursue it to the bitter end, not realizing that the good we are pursuing has turned on us and become evil before our eyes.

The whole thing reminds me of a line from the classic western "The Outlaw Josey Wales." A brutal, despicable northern officer has sworn to bring in the hero, Josey Wales, and has pressed one of Wales' friends into helping him. At one point in the movie he talks about all the other outlaws they'll go after when they've gotten Wales. The other man protests, "Once we get Wales it ends." But the evil man responds, totally sincere, "Doing right ain't got no end."

Are you willing to let God declare what is good and what is evil? Or do you insist on defining that for yourself? Be careful, because you might be surprised by some of what God labels good. And what he calls evil. He might look at you and say, "You are my child, in you I am well pleased." How would you deal with that? He might look at people you reject and despise and say the same thing to them. And what then?

So far we have been dealing with the word "good" in ethical terms. But there is another point to be made about goodness in Genesis 1. In the philosophy of the Greeks and some other cultures, physical matter was viewed as evil. Or at least under suspicion. For the Greeks, the spirit was good, physical matter was bad. Many Bible readers today have bought into a similar idea. But the Bible will have none of it. According to the Bible, God looked at the physical creation he had made and declared it good. Not just once but many times. When he created human beings with physical bodies, he said they are very good.

The physical stuff of creation, according to God, is good. Matter is good. Rocks and trees, lakes and mountains, dirt and flowers, you and me. Our substance is good.

Also, the divide between spirit and matter that was so important to the Greeks isn't really present in Genesis. In the Bible, there is no real division between the spiritual and the physical. Both can be twisted and do evil. But both are created by a good God, and they reflect his goodness. Thinking biblically about it, we are both physical and spiritual at the same time. You can't really separate the two.

Time Out: How do you read Genesis?

The first dozen chapters of Genesis probably spark more controversy in our culture than any other part of the Bible. Creationists bang the drum for God getting it all done in a literal week; evolutionists roll their eyes and dismiss the whole thing as mythology. Advocates of intelligent design try to find a middle road and take the whole thing as some kind of wider parable that assures us there really is a driving force behind the whole business. The average church-goer is stuck somewhere on this spectrum, maybe believing that each day played out like Genesis 1 says, maybe believing it's just intended to assure us in general terms that God created the world and it didn't come about by accident. People on the extremes tend to fight about this creation debate in school board meetings and on talk radio shows, in books and interviews and occasionally in a face-to-face debate.

The whole thing generates a lot more heat than light. Speaking as a Minnesotan writing this as winter is approaching, I still don't want that kind of heat.

A "literal" reading of Genesis 1-12 brings up a few questions. Having spent seven years in youth ministry and a few more decades as a pastor, I've heard most of the questions that go with these chapters. Here are a few of the best:

- What existed before all this story started?
- How long ago is "in the beginning"?
- Do snakes really talk?
- Of course the classic, Did Adam & Eve have belly buttons?
- Where did Cain's wife come from?

- Why did Cain found a city if there were a dozen
  people on earth?
- What about cave men? Where do they fit?
- What about dinosaurs?
- What about the fossil record?
- How could the earth really be repopulated from the
  animals on one boat?
- How could a wooden boat the size of the ark hold
  together in heavy seas?
- Could people really live 900 years or more?

And of course there are more.

These questions are all very entertaining. But they totally miss
the point. I'm about to give away my bias, so pay attention.

All these questions assume a post-Enlightenment view of the
Genesis stories. Post-Enlightenment thinking says you get to
know something by taking it apart, like a toaster. You can
disassemble your toaster and figure out what connects to what
and why it works. (Please unplug it before trying this at
home.) On non-living things, this works fine, though I always
had trouble getting things put back together again, and
frequently they didn't work quite the same as they did before I
took them apart.

But this way of knowing doesn't work so well on living
things. Your cat, for example. You can't take the cat apart and
put it back together again. You have to live with the cat in
order to know it, and the more time you spend with it the
better you'll understand it. (Reading a little Kipling might help
as well: "I am the cat who walks by himself, and all places are
alike to me.")

The Enlightenment, that period of time when we believed that
pure logic and rationality would solve all our problems and
Science held all the answers, has made it very hard for you

and me to understand the Bible. I think to understand the Bible
we have to live in relationship with it, get to know it, treat it
like a living thing.

In short, I don't find it helpful to dissect Genesis in order to
understand it. It isn't helpful to me to ask questions of truth
and falsehood, accuracy or inaccuracy. I find it much more
helpful to live with the stories and relate to these stories like a
living thing, because I believe that's exactly what they are.

As I live with the Bible, I find that these are stories about me.
I learn about myself as I read Genesis. Who am I? Where do I
come from? Why was I created? What is my relationship to
the rest of creation? Why do I do the things I do? Why do the
people around me do the things they do?

So in short, Genesis isn't about what happened back then. It's
about what happened at my house this afternoon. Reading it
for the sake of ancient history might be fun and entertaining in
a speculative kind of way, but it totally misses the point.

I know many of you are thinking, "Yeah, but…" and you're
going to tell me it's accurate, or it's mythological, or whatever.
I know. I do. But for the moment, let it go and listen to what
the story says about you and what you see when you look out
your window, or across the dinner table, or on the evening
news.

Curve Ball

Okay, now that I've made my claim about how Genesis is all about what happened at my house yesterday afternoon, that it totally misses the point of Genesis to speculate about what happened back when (I still hold to those points of view, by the way) I need to share with you a book I've been reading.

I was at a bookstore not long ago looking for something by N.T. Wright (highly recommend) and they didn't have the book I was looking for. But I did run across something else. It's called *The Genesis Enigma* and it's written by Andrew Parker, an evolutionary biologist from England. He subscribes to Darwinian evolution and writes rather tongue-in-cheek about how the church has been on the wrong side of so many scientific advances. But the subtitle of this book is "Why the Bible is scientifically accurate." Interesting.

Parker's claim to fame is his research into the evolution of the eye, which he says first appeared in trilobites about 521 million years ago. He writes in great detail about the whole process of evolution from the Big Bang down through the formation of the solar system, the earth, and the appearance of life. For a non-scientist like me, he writes very accessibly. He not only tells what scientists believe happened, but also about the scientists through history who made the discoveries that lead us in these directions. It's a fascinating read.

The thrust of his book, though, is that he makes a detailed and specific set of claims that the Genesis 1 creation account is matched in great detail with evolutionary chronology. The deeper he dug into the resemblance between the two sequences, the more mystified he became. How could a desert people like the Israelites come up with a mythology that tells about the appearance of life in exactly the same order (according to Parker) that evolutionary biology does? He has finally come to the conclusion that this sequence in Genesis 1 is strong evidence for the divine inspiration of the Bible. Parker himself is uncomfortable with his conclusions. It's almost funny to read when he gets squirmy about claiming divine inspiration. But he follows the evidence resolutely where it leads him (I skipped ahead and read the end of the book already.)

There are some holes in Parker's argument that even I could drive a truck through. But those holes don't necessarily threaten his overall assertion. He's convinced that there is an uncanny resemblance between the chronology proposed by evolutionary biologists and the sequence of creation in Genesis.

So while I don't believe arguing about what happened back then is particularly helpful when it comes to Genesis (I still say that's missing the point) it is fascinating to me to think that God might have been planting seeds in that account through which Andrew Parker and others like him might someday be drawn to know him. Good stuff.

Boundaries: "Then God separated…"

Have you noticed how much separating happens in Genesis 1? God separates light from darkness, heavens from earth, land from water, and on it goes. In our culture today many people make God all about reconciliation, by which they mean that it doesn't matter if you're this or that, we should all get along. I'm all for getting along, but God is about relationship. And relationships require good boundaries. So as God creates order out of chaos, he first creates separation.

A few years ago there was a popular book called *Boundaries* that spawned a series of sequels and workbooks and individual studies. These books were helpful to many, many people because when our lives are chaotic, one of the first casualties is that we fail to have good boundaries. Who I am and who you are gets blurred and I end up owning your baggage and you end up suffering for my mistakes. Boundaries help us have healthy relationships.

So what does it mean to have relationship? It means that heaven is not earth, land is not water, I am not you. But our eyes and our hearts are drawn to the places where what has been separated meets. We look to the horizon. We play at the beach. We adore images of lovers holding hands, lips meeting, a head on a shoulder, the electricity of eye contact. Even in the natural world, life is most abundant in the transition zone where one kind of terrain meets another. But in order for that to happen, the river needs to be different from the forest needs to be different from the prairie.

We don't necessarily like it when God separates things, because when he does he also names them. When God names me for what I am, it makes me a little uncomfortable. The truth can be hard to take. A professor of mine once said that the most offensive message the church can speak to the world is, "Your sin is forgiven for Jesus' sake." I've seen this myself. Many people's reaction is most often to indignantly say, "My sin? What do you mean, 'my sin'? Who are you to label me a sinner?" The message of reconciliation gets lost because the world is offended at being separated and named. We don't want to hear it.

I would like to believe lots of things about myself that are just not true. I would like to believe I'm right, I'm logical, I'm pure. But while these things may sometimes be true of me, often I am wrong, I'm irrational, I'm polluted. So sometimes God speaks the truth about me. He might use the voice of his written word in the Bible or the voice of my wife or the voice of my coworkers. When he speaks the truth about me and contradicts what I want to believe about myself, I cringe. But if I reject this word, if I refuse to see what is true about myself, I remain cut off from relationship with God and with others. If I refuse to recognize the boundary that fences me in, I can never come up against it in order to have relationship with anyone beyond myself.

In short, what God is doing in this act of separating and naming creation is an act of love. He creates the universe, including you and me, in such a way that we can come to the end of ourselves. It is there, at the end of ourselves, that we can have a relationship with the God who is beyond us.

Reconciliation

Continuing the thought from the last chapter:

By God's grace, you are not me. I have my own baggage, my own strengths, my own sins, and you have yours. You own yours and I own mine, and perhaps we can live in relationship. If we don't own our own issues, relationships cannot happen because they are chaos. I become simply a projection of your inner garbage, and you are a tool I use for my own ends. This need for appropriate boundaries is true in any relationship, whether we're talking about friendship or marriage or a relationship with God.

And sometimes in the wisdom of God the separation needs to be greater. The sun cannot come into contact with the earth, or life on this planet would end. That relationship has to be distant. The polar ice caps cannot rub up against the tropical seashore, or both will be destroyed. It's part of the order of a diverse creation.

In some human relationships, too, we recognize that it is wiser to maintain a distance. Occasionally I will talk with someone who has been deeply wounded, and they struggle to forgive the one who wounded them. They somehow believe that if they forgive that person, they have to open themselves again to that relationship in a way that may well put them at risk to be wounded all over again. Sometimes that is necessary and appropriate. But often forgiveness means letting go of the hurt, and letting go of the desire for vengeance, and then living at an appropriate distance.

So what does "reconciliation" mean? In the Bible, this is a huge theme. Paul, who wrote about a third of the New Testament, writes about this in his letter to the Ephesians.

Here's how Eugene Peterson in *The Message* brings Paul's words into modern English:

> The Messiah has made things up between us so that we're now together on this, both non-Jewish outsiders and Jewish insiders. He tore down the wall we used to keep each other at a distance. He repealed the law code that had become so clogged with fine print and footnotes that it hindered more than it helped. Then he started over. Instead of continuing with two groups of people separated by centuries of animosity and suspicion, he created a new kind of human being, a fresh start for everybody.
>
> Christ brought us together through his death on the cross. The Cross got us to embrace, and that was the end of the hostility. Christ came and preached peace to you outsiders and peace to us insiders. He treated us as equals, and so made us equals. Through him we both share the same Spirit and have equal access to the Father. (from Ephesians 2)

First of all, reconciliation does not change the fact that we are separate. But it introduces a relationship where before there was only a "wall we used to keep each other at a distance." Paul is first speaking here to the separation between Jews and Gentiles and all the rules the Jews had developed to create a chasm of separation between the two. Paul is not saying that from here on out there will be no such thing as Jews and Gentiles. Rather, he is saying that what they have in common is greater than what separates them. The two groups together are restored to relationship with God, and to each other, through the sacrifice of Jesus on the cross.

We can extrapolate this to other separations in our world. When we are alienated from an individual, or when we isolate and insulate ourselves from a group of people (homeless people, for example, or illegal aliens, or people of another race or culture), the blood of Christ brings us together on common ground at the foot of the cross. What we have in common (our dependence on God's grace at the cross) is greater than what separates us, and makes relationship possible.

When we begin to grasp this idea that God has created difference, that God has created separation, we begin to delight in it. This distinction is part of the goodness of creation, and we get in trouble when we blur the categories. When I recognize that I am different from another person, I can begin to value their unique perspectives and learn from the things they do or believe that are different. It doesn't mean that I should give up what I do or believe. Instead, I can learn from them and value them for who they are.

This has huge implications for how Jesus' followers live in the world. We do not discard the world, but we also don't give in and become like the world. This is the world, after all, that "God so loved." Jesus came to this world to build a relationship, to make reconciliation possible.

This business of boundaries and separation works out in more subtle ways as well. Think for a moment about all the creativity God has exercised to give you abundant life here and now. It's not just about giving you the ability to earn a living, though that's important. You benefit here and now from hundreds, maybe thousands, of years of human migration. You have ancestors who worked to make your life possible, whether you know their names or not. Wars and economic disruption and boom and bust have all moved through the years to give you the life you have today. What is the history of the land on which you live, even if you live in an apartment building? That land carries God's creativity over the centuries.

Too often we get hung up on the damage we've suffered in the past. In Acts 17 Paul preaches that God has set the boundaries of our dwelling places and the times in which we live. He's done this so we will seek him, for he is not far from any of us.

Can we let go of "this hard thing happened to me" and move on to "God, what are you up to?" There are lots of difficult events in your history and mine. Can we learn to look at the past without flinching? It's difficult. Famine, abuse, destruction, desolation. God redeems our difficult histories to give us abundant life in the present if we will let him.

In the final analysis, reconciliation requires that we surrender to life within the boundaries God has set for us. We accept that our life is here, now. We give up on the fantasy of some other time, some other place, some other set of circumstances.

Only then can we say, "Lord, what are you up to in my life?" and eagerly accept the answer.

Awe: Genesis 1:14-19

Have you noticed how the word "awesome" has been stolen? It used to be if something was "awesome" that meant it shook you to your core. Now it means next to nothing.

I don't know another word, however, to explain what happens in this passage. God has created vegetation. Life has begun. Now he sets himself to create an orderly system of lights that will govern days, and seasons, and years. (I read a book once that claimed the zodiac was originally designed by God to point the way to Christ, not to predict whether you were going to have a good day or not. Fascinating.)

But the piece that is awesome here hasn't shown up yet. Hang on.

Ever since growing up in northern Minnesota far away from the bright city lights, I've been fascinated by the night sky. Look up on a cold January night when there's no moon and you can see thousands and thousands of stars. The Milky Way looks like a bright ribbon of light across the cold sky. Bundle up and watch long enough and you begin to see the entire sky pinwheeling around Polaris like some gigantic nightly dance, which of course means that it's really the earth that is dancing some marvelous pirouette so we can see the whole sky every 24 hours.

Astronomers tell us that our own galaxy, the Milky Way, has about 100 billion stars organized in a pinwheel formation with two arms extended from a bulging disc at the core. The Milky Way sits in the center of a group of "satellite galaxies." These are sort of our close friends in this part of the universe. Farther away are many other galaxies. In fact, roughly another 100 billion galaxies. Do the multiplication and you come up with an amazing number of stars. Now it begins to fit the word "awesome." If you could count the stars, you would need somewhere in the neighborhood of a 10 with twenty-two zeroes after it. It is a number far greater than we can imagine. In 1995, the Hubble Space Telescope spent ten days focusing on a tiny fragment of sky near the handle of the Big Dipper. If you had a friend stand 75 feet away from you and hold up a dime, that's how much of the sky Hubble used. Taking picture after picture of this same slice of sky in various formats, Hubble looked deeper and deeper into the sky to see farther and farther and capture objects that were far too faint to be seen by our eyes. Scientists cobbled together the multiple images of this same tiny fragment of sky.

This dime-sized image shows more than 1500 galaxies. Not stars, galaxies. They hang like tiny Christmas ornaments in that one core sample of space. Each itty bitty dot is millions of light years across and contains billions of stars. The scientists who organized this project intentionally chose a portion of the sky that would have few or no stars in the foreground to interfere with seeing all these galaxies. Astronomers tell us that the density of the universe, in other words the distribution of galaxies, is roughly the same in all directions from us. So if you could get rid of the foreground lights and look all over the night sky, and if your eyes were sufficiently sensitive, this is what you would see in every direction. Millions of billions of galaxies.

Genesis describes the creation of our planet, and our sun, and the lights that God created to help us gauge times and seasons. Then almost as an afterthought the writer adds, "He also made the stars." As in, oh, yeah, I almost forgot to mention it.

Our God is *awesome.*

Space and Life and Beauty

When I first wrote this chapter, I was on a retreat at a camp in central Minnesota. I had the privilege of staying in a new log A-frame building with an amazing stone fireplace. The cathedral ceilings and open beam construction, the intricate ship models and just overall amazingness (that's my daughter's word) of the place warmed my heart and gave me a sense of joy and contentment when I walked in the door.

I heard an interview with theologian John Polkinghorne many years ago. One of the major themes in the interview was the presence of beauty in creation.

Why is beauty so important to us? Why do open spaces or beautiful settings move us so powerfully? Or for that matter, why do we like cathedral ceilings? They're terribly impractical from the perspective of heating, dusting, and use of space. Yet there was something in that space where I stayed in the retreat center that drew my heart upward toward the open-beamed ceiling and outward, through the expansive windows, to the broad stretch of lake ice that opened out for miles, starting at the bottom of the bluff below me. Beauty is important.

As you read the orderly account of creation in Genesis 1, you can begin to sense that beauty is dear to God's heart. I don't think I'm stretching things to say that beauty matters to God. From the intricate beauty of the stars to the majestic movement of a pod of orcas to the wheeling flight of pelicans, God enjoys beauty.

Part of what makes something beautiful, I believe, is the interplay between space and abundance. "Abundance" might not be the right word; I'm thinking of the words here in the creation story like "teeming" and "filled" and "variety" and such. Or where in John 10 Jesus says, "I came that they might have life, and have it abundantly" (ESV). The night sky would not be beautiful without the backdrop of a starless void. The unbearable beauty of falling in love would be less if we had never known loneliness.

I remember the joy of finding a patch of blackberries in a forest when I lived near Seattle. That joy was only memorable because it was a dry year and the blackberry bushes that filled the road ditches and the vacant lots were bare. But somehow this patch had found an underground source of water, and the berries were full and rich and luscious and the juices dripped down my chin. Beautiful. When space and abundant life are arranged in a way that balances them and sets each off against the other, it is beautiful.

This idea of beauty, that it is about the presence of abundant life starkly contrasted against its opposite so that we can actually see it, tells us something about the heart of God. God is all about giving life. The chaotic void becomes the arena for God to create. The empty world becomes God's garden. The quiet garden needs voices. God brings life, and life abundant, to fill the emptiness of the void. God uses the contrast to heighten beauty.

And we are created in God's image. (We'll have more to say about this soon.) So we go looking for life, especially when our lives seem to have become a tepid canvas without form or beauty to fill them. We seek out all kinds of abundance to fill the empty depths of our souls. New cars. New careers. New lovers. New addictions. We turn to all these things hoping for something that will bring life to us. Most of what we seek out is a useless attempt to find meaning. Like the old country song, we are looking for love in all the wrong places. In the end, instead of a lovely light, our lives are just a dim bulb.

The Bible tells us that it is in Jesus that we find life that lights up the darkened space of our days. Beautiful. In Jesus there is light, John's gospel tells us. And that light can be life for all people.

If you're looking for more on God's enjoyment of his beautiful creation, just for kicks take a look at Job 38-41. Wow!

Bring Forth: Genesis 1

Back to that evolutionary biology book, *The Genesis Enigma*. I found it so thought-provoking. Not because I agree with all of it, but because I haven't thought about things from some of these perspectives, and it challenges me. I've never had a long conversation about Genesis 1 with an evolutionary biologist, and that's what this book amounts to.

One of the ideas that Parker throws out is the term the King James translates "bring forth" or the NIV translates "produce." It's there in Genesis 1, verses 11, 20, 21, and 24. As in "Let the earth bring forth" vegetation, sea creatures, and land animals. Interesting that God speaks of the earth bringing these forms of life to creation. Even more interesting that the next time this word appears is in Genesis 3:16-18. There it refers to the woman giving birth to children. Hm.

So, at the risk of yanking some chains, does this imply that God uses another device or method to create these things? No one here is disputing that God is creator, but by what method does he create? If God says, "Let the earth bring forth..." does that imply that there is some earthly tool used to create these things? Like, perhaps, an evolutionary process overseen and guided by God as a creative tool?

I'm not arguing for a synthesis of science and religion, not in any way. But I think too often those who see themselves as the guardians of the Bible (as though it needed guarding) are quick to say, "No! God created it like this because this is what I believe." The danger, of course, is that we look only at our beliefs and not at what the Bible actually says.

"Let the earth bring forth life." Why would God say it that way? Why would the writer(s) of Genesis write it down this way? I don't want to make a mountain out of a molehill (no matter how either one was created) but it's enough to make you think. And maybe that's the point.

The Image of God: Genesis 1:26-31

Whole books could be written on this passage alone. There is so much packed into these few verses. What does it mean that humans are created in the image of God? What does it mean that we are created male and female in that image? What does it mean for us to exercise dominion, to rule over the rest of creation? The questions go on and on.

Michelangelo portrayed God in the image of man on the ceiling of the Sistine Chapel. That is, he extrapolated from human form and chose to portray God as a bearded old man, holding out his finger to create Adam. Visually, the image is stunning. Taken literally, it leaves something to be desired.

In the 1970's, on the cover of his album "Aqualung," Jethro Tull stated that "Man created God in his own image…" This is a danger we must always be aware of. We picture God as we are. If I am petty and fearful, I picture God this way. If I keep score, guess what my God does? If I am judgmental, or play favorites, or if I am unfair, guess what? We limit God by perceiving him through our own image. Jesus even alluded to this in some of his parables.

So how do we get this business of being created in the image of God in proper perspective? Elsewhere the Bible makes pretty clear that being made in the image of God is not about noses, fingers, eyebrows, or any other physical feature. "God is Spirit," Jesus said in John 4. But there is something about God that we imitate, an image that we bear that reflects the Creator.

In ancient origin stories, it was fairly common to talk about the king as "the image of God." The Pharaoh in Egypt, for example, was a descendant of the gods. One of the unique things about the way Genesis talks about the image of God is that not just the king, but all people are created in the image of God.

Not just males, either. The Bible has been much abused as a chauvinistic and misogynistic document over the years. But read it carefully and you'll be amazed how the Bible consistently empowers both men and women.

Being created in the image of God moves in so many dimensions. Our use of language is one example. Just as God speaks, we are users of language. As God rules over his creation, we are called to exercise dominion over creation. (More on this later.) God is up to something in this world. We might almost say he is on a mission. Specifically we see in Genesis how God creates a plan that will take millennia to unfold. His plan is to deal with the damage that sin does to his beloved creation. We are created in the image of God, with a great capacity for mission. At our best, our mission is a part of and supports God's mission. We are privileged to work with God, bearing his image as we pursue the mission he shares with us.

Another aspect of bearing the image of God is glory. As God is glorious, so there is a beauty and a glory to human beings. This is why advertisers use pictures of people to advertise products. Because visual images of humans attract us.

One more note about being created in the image of God. In the ancient world, it was common practice for a king or emperor to set up a statue of himself in the farthest reaches of his domain. That image was a reminder of the emperor's power and rule. It reminded the citizens who they belonged to. So as humans are created in the image of God, we are a reminder to all creation (and to each other) that we belong to God, that though we may not see him, he is the emperor. And someday he will come back to us in person.

There are all these facets to being created in God's image.
Jesus put a fine point on it in Mark's gospel. He was asked if it
was right to pay taxes to Caesar (the faraway emperor) and he
asked to see a Roman coin. "Whose image is on the coin?" he
asked.

"Caesar's," they answered.

Jesus went straight to the creation story. "Give Caesar the
things that are Caesar's," he said. "Give to God the things that
are God's." In other words, since you are made in God's
image, don't hold yourself back from God. You belong to him.

Here is perhaps the deepest aspect of being created in God's
image: We are designed for relationships. It becomes clearer
and clearer as you wade through the Bible that God is all
about relationships. He starts them, refines them, recasts and
revises and reforms them. Over and over again we see God
making covenants to try to define relationships. Abraham and
Sarah. Jacob. Moses. David. Jesus brought relationships into
sharp focus. "I no longer call you servants, but friends," he
told his disciples. Even his opening line, "Come, follow me,"
was an invitation to relationship.

Think of how you became the person you are today. Without
question, your strengths and your character were formed in the
forge of relationships. Who was a role model, a hero, for you?
Who wounded you so deeply you have never recovered? Who
limps along with you from day to day, sharing the joys and
sorrows of your life? We are relational beings. None of us can
live without relationships, not even the most solitary hermit.
We are constantly interacting and influencing those around us.
In the last couple decades, the entire internet has been
dominated by social media, which is all about relationships.

It is in relationships we find our deepest joys, our most wrenching grief, our most twisted wrongs. It is in relationships that we experience the fullest expression of our created potential. We cannot escape this. Relationships cripple us and redeem us and fulfill us. As much as we would sometimes like to live totally independent, we cannot do so. We must not do so. We are created for relationships.

This is no accident. This is God's design in creation. We need to live in community. We need to depend on people, and have them rely on us. Trust. Compassion. Humor. Interdependence. Comfort. Challenge. All of these words are lived out in relationships.

Shortly we will see that it is in our relationships, too, that we experience our greatest brokenness. But for the moment, suffice it to say that God has created us in his image, meaning that we are created for relationships. This is where our lives will be shaped, our characters formed. If we are to find our place in creation, it will depend on the recognition that God has created us for relationship with himself, with other humans, and with the rest of creation. In that web of intricately interconnected ties we find ourselves and learn who we are.

So much in our world is based on this idea that we are created in the image of God. Every western culture that believes humans have inherent worth gets that belief from this biblical teaching. When in the United States Declaration of Independence we read that "we hold these truths to be self-evident, that all men are created equal, and that they are endowed by their Creator with certain inalienable rights," that concept grows from Genesis 1.

Male and Female

Here, for the first time in the Bible, we find the differentiation of genders. From this point forward, the distinction between male and female will be huge. We cannot begin to imagine creation without gender differences, and rightly so. Maleness and femaleness are created into the very core of our being.

When I was much younger, many of my teachers said that gender was just something about the surface. Being male or female was simply an accident of tissues, not something that made a core difference. It was only a cultural bias, we were told, that made a big deal out of being male or female. I suppose at the time (in the late 1970's) this was a natural outgrowth of the push for women's liberation, equal pay for equal work, and all those worthy goals that I fully support. But as in so many cases, the pendulum swung so far that we said things that were unbelievable. Like, "boys and girls are exactly the same, it is just their plumbing that is different." Hogwash.

Listen to the conversation between parents of young children. Those that tend girls face a completely different set of challenges from those who are herding boys. There are commonalities, of course. But boys and girls behave differently, in ways that go far beyond conditioning.

Developmental biologists and psychologists have recognized this all along. There are biological differences in the brains of male and female that distinguish them. It's about far more than plumbing.

In our world today we face a plethora of challenges to this idea of maleness and femaleness. Many people describe themselves as non-binary, or transgender, or a host of other terms. On an individual level, it is important to listen more than we dictate. But when we look at the broad scope of creation, and certainly at the broad scope of humanity, we are created male and female. I sat and listened to a college student once who was struggling through these issues. She had friends who were defining themselves and choosing their pronouns and all the rest. She loved her friends deeply, respected them, and honored their wishes. "But," she finally said, "I've studied a lot of biology. And gender is a thing."

Genesis says,

> So God created human beings in his own image.
> In the image of God he created them;
> male and female he created them.

Once we get into Genesis 2 things will look a little different. There we'll see the man created first and the woman later, and this will lead us to a whole new set of reflections about relationships. Even Genesis 2, as we will see, gives a sense of balance and equality between genders. It is important to recognize that Genesis first mentions gender in a symmetrical, balanced way, not in a hierarchical system in which males are inherently better than females or vice versa. We need each other and we are interrelated in the plan of God. Gender bias, male domination, misogyny, and many other evils will appear in scripture. But those evils are not here. In our creation we are together, united in bearing the image of God.

What do we do with the God-given gift of gender? God gives clear instructions: "Be fruitful and multiply." Fruitfulness is an idea that will come back again and again, and it applies to far more than bearing children. Then we are told to "exercise dominion" or "rule" over the rest of creation. While our fallen minds immediately jump to the concept of domination, this idea doesn't necessarily stick to these verses. If we are created in the image of God, what does it mean to rule? What does it mean to exercise dominion (literally, "lordship") over creation?

It means that we exercise authority in the same way God exercises authority. How does this happen? Jesus is our example. He is the "visible expression of the invisible God" (see Colossians 1:15). How did Jesus exercise authority? John's gospel describes Jesus knowing his authority, knowing his status as God, and yet stripping down to wash his followers' muddy feet. (See John 13.) Take a look at Philippians 2. There we see that because he is Lord, Jesus is willing to empty himself for the sake of his beloved creation. He is willing to pick up a towel and do the servant's job. His lordship is based on loving servanthood.

When we believe that our dominion over creation means that we can rape the land, strip mine the minerals, abuse the atmosphere, and build shopping malls on the wetlands, we have totally missed what it means to be created in the image of God. Yes, God will allow us to behave in these ways. But we will reap what we sow.

In the same way, when we look at what it means to be male and female, we treat each other in this same sense of loving servanthood. We tend each other and nurture each other as the bearers of the image of God. We get down on our knees with a towel and a basin. We empty ourselves, not because we are worthless. Far from it. We serve because this is the character of the God whose image we bear.

Part of what humans are given together as male and female is dominion. This is a servant rule given to us by God. It is not the right to exploit creation.

Why do we not see ourselves ruling over creation? We see ourselves frustrated more often. Our dominion gets twisted and polluted. Why?

Oswald Chambers said it this way:

> God created man to be master of the life in
> the earth and sea and sky, and the reason he
> is not is because he took the law into his
> own hands, and became master of himself,
> but of nothing else.

We will have to deal with our grasping sin. But first we need
to work through another chapter that describes God's creation
in detail.

Fruitful

Over the last few years I have been astounded by the number of times the Bible talks about bearing fruit or fruitfulness. The first time I heard this theme lifted up was at a church staff retreat when one of the speakers who spent time with us talked about the difference between productivity and fruitfulness.

Have you ever thought about this?

At first they don't seem so different. If I'm working hard, I'm making things happen, doing my job, I'm producing something. I'm "bearing fruit." It's kind of a poetic, biblical way to say the same thing. Right?

Maybe not so much.

The question at heart is, whose work is getting done? When I produce something, I am the driver, the decision maker, the agenda owner. I'm the one making something happen. Think how we use that word. If you are a productive member of society, you are valuable, you're worth keeping around because of what you make or do. Many jobs include an evaluation based on productivity.

I live in Minnesota, where nearly everyone is a Vikings fan. Minnesota Vikings fans are used to getting all excited as our team enters the playoffs yet again. "Maybe this year!" we think. Then in the first, or on really good years the second, round of the playoffs, our boys choke. It's predictable, like cold weather in January.

After that playoff loss a few years ago, one of the local pundits observed that productivity in Minnesota would be way down today due to all the after-the-fact quarterbacking that would happen around the water coolers across the state. Productivity is (duh!) about what we produce. If I am distracted, depressed, unfocused, talking too much, or in any other way off-center, I will be less productive. If I am a grief-stricken Vikings fan, I will not be very productive today.

Is this different from fruitfulness?

Think about the picture. A tree doesn't decide what kind of fruit to bear. That is encoded in its DNA. A tree doesn't decide where to bear fruit. That is decided by the "accident" of where a seed is dropped or a cutting established. A tree doesn't will the fruit to appear. The tree simply does what it does, growing deep roots into the soil and leaves that reach to the sunlight, and fruit happens. God has created the tree through a bunch of natural processes and sets those same natural processes in place so that the tree can bear fruit.

Is it possible that the fruit God wants you to bear is not the same as the difference you want to make? Is it possible that you are bearing fruit, or God is preparing you to bear fruit, in a way that is off your radar, in an arena where you don't even realize you have an impact?

One of the worst tragedies in this world is that of committed Christians who are out to make a difference for God but who neglect the places they have been planted. They're tilting at windmills while neglecting their spouses, children, and neighborhoods. Generation after generation sees "great" Christian leaders who rise up to change the world, but then we find that their foundations are made of sand. They're striving for productivity rather than bearing fruit.

Where have you been planted? What kind of fruit has God created you to bear? How have you bought into the lie of productivity? We will touch on this again later.

Let's take this idea of fruitfulness and apply it to a specific situation. I'm always intrigued by people who take scripture and apply it to stuff in the present day. As you know if you've read this far, that's my whole approach to Genesis. And I cordially dislike the practice of making Genesis all about what happened back then.

I was reading an amazing book (re-reading, actually, and worth every moment) about what churches should be doing with their time and energy. If you're in any kind of church leadership or if you are interested at all in churches or if you despise churches and love Jesus, you ought to read *Organic Church* by Neil Cole. You may not agree with him in all details but he'll certainly make you think hard.

Here is a lengthy quote that lays out some challenging ideas and ends with this concept of fruitfulness, in a very poignant way. Most of Cole's book is an answer to the problem he lays out in this quote:

> American Christianity is dying. Our future is in serious jeopardy. We are deathly ill and don't even know it. Our illness has so saturated our institutions that we are not healthy enough to live beyond the present generation. Our only hope is to try to keep current organizations alive for as long as possible, by any means possible. This is the mentality in Christian 'churchianity.' Many institutions are holding on to life support, fearing that death is the end of us. Do you think I am overstating our condition? Then it is even more evidence of how bad off we are. Look at the facts.
>
> The Southern Baptists have said that only 4 percent of the churches in America will plant a

daughter church. That means that 96 percent of the conventional churches in America will never give birth. On the basis of experience, I believe this statistic is true. Even worse, I suspect that the majority of the 4 percent that do give birth will do so with an 'unwanted pregnancy' which we call a church split.

Many people think this state of affairs is fine. I have heard people say, 'We have plenty of churches. There are churches all over the place that sit empty, so why start new ones? We don't need more churches, but better ones.' Can you imagine making such a statement about people? 'We have plenty of people. We don't need more people, just better ones. Why have more babies?' This short-range thinking is only interested in the here and now and does not think there are long-term consequences for living selfish lives.

… Imagine the headlines if it were suddenly discovered that 96 percent of the women in America were no longer fertile and could not have babies. We would instantly know two things. First, this is not natural, so there is something wrong with their health. Second, we would also know that the future is in serious jeopardy. This is the state of the church in America right now. It is that serious, and we need to take heed.

We need a new form of church that can be fruitful and multiply. Many of our churches do not even want to multiply. (From *Organic Church*, pages 91-92)

So what would it look like if churches were fruitful, instead of productive? (Lots of churches aren't even productive, but that's another matter.) What about pastors? Or Christians in general? When Jesus talked about what he dreamed for us, he used this image of fruitfulness in a very powerful way. (See John 15).

Do you suppose that Genesis 1 even has something to say to churches? How about that.

Thanksgiving: Genesis 2:1-3

When I made my living as a preacher, I cordially disliked
Thanksgiving. Not the action, but the holiday. Okay, that's not
true. I liked the holiday, but I struggled with preaching on
Thanksgiving.

Real gratitude is one of the most enjoyable things I have
experienced. To be grateful to someone is to know your
connection with them, to acknowledge your joyful dependence
on them, and to recognize the blessing that has come from that
relationship. Gratitude is fun. So "giving thanks" is a huge
part of our relationship with God, and it is probably
impossible to do too much "giving thanks" in our prayers. We
are absolutely dependent on God for everything we have and
are. As we recognize that dependence, we can experience
great joy. So I love giving thanks. My prayers almost always
start out with thanks to God for something.

But I disliked preaching on Thanksgiving because there is a
tremendous temptation as a preacher to say, in some way,
"You should be thankful!" This gracious opportunity for joyful
dependence becomes instead a law-laden guilt trip that says,
"You're a self-centered boor; you own too many toys and you
spend too much of your income on yourself and the least you
could do is be thankful for the ability to overindulge." I know
preachers don't really say that at Thanksgiving, but it feels
like it sometimes. Anytime we use the word "should" we are
probably dropping cement blocks of Law on people's
shoulders.

A friend of mine used to say, "Don't should on me."
Thanksgiving is closely tied to rest. We often approach both
these topics from a perspective of law. We think, "I should be

thankful. I should rest more." We burden ourselves with God's good gifts in a way he does not intend. And it's not helpful.

There's the danger with this text, Genesis 2:1-3. God finishes his work of creating the universe in six days, and on the seventh day he rests. So he makes Day 7 holy forever. This verse became the root of the Jews' Sabbath observance, the root of the tradition of not working on Sundays, blue laws, and all the rest. We see this text as normative for our own scheduling. We recognize (and the scientific establishment has verified) the importance of taking a day out of seven to rest. This is a gracious gift from a loving God.

But it's very easy, especially these days, to beat ourselves up by how unrestful we are. Biblical teachers and leaders, myself included, harp on our busy schedules, overcommitments, scattered lives. We fail to "be still and know that I am God," as Psalm 46 says. We flog ourselves with our busy-ness. Mea culpa, mea culpa, mea maxima culpa, we say (from the old Latin liturgy, I am guilty, I am guilty, I am most guilty). Then we go back to our calendars, cars, schedules, cell phones, and all the rest of the accouterments that clutter our lives and keep us from rest.

Maybe beating ourselves up doesn't work. Maybe it doesn't change things. Maybe we like being busy and this idea of rest scares us a little bit.

So the question I have to ask when I bump up against these verses in Genesis is, what am I missing? Like a kid filling himself on Doritos before an amazing Thanksgiving dinner is laid out on the table, have I filled my life so full that there's no room for what God wants? And what is it God wants?

If you start thinking about this and start to beat yourself up, go do something else for a while. Forget it. But does the idea of rest sounds like a cup of cold water to a thirsty person? Are you dying from clutter and overcommitment and longing for peace? Have you been staying in bed three more minutes and wishing it could be another hour, not to sleep, just to relax? If being busy is hurting you and you're ready to consider alternatives I have a recommendation. It's a book by an amazing writer, Mark Buchanan. He has written a book called *The Rest of God* (pun intended) that takes on this whole idea of resting in a new and different way. As an example, when he talks about setting aside a day for rest, the first question that comes up is, "What can't I do on that day?" Can I go shopping? Can I mow the lawn? Can I read a book? Can I cook supper? I really like his answer. He says his rule of thumb is, if it's a day of rest, don't do anything you have to do. So if you don't have to mow the lawn, you can do it. If you don't have to go shopping and that would be a restful thing for you, do it. If cooking supper is a delight that gives you life and you don't need to do it (you have options), go ahead.

I like it. I think Jesus is big into our resting. He often told his disciples to go away and rest. He took time alone to rest. When he faced a crisis or had been in the middle of intensity for too long, he rested.

What am I missing? Have I scheduled rest out of my life?

> Then Jesus said, "Come to me, all of you
> who are weary and carry heavy burdens, and
> I will give you rest. Take my yoke upon you.
> Let me teach you, because I am humble and
> gentle at heart, and you will find rest for
> your souls. For my yoke is easy to bear, and
> the burden I give you is light." (Matthew
> 11:28-30)

Genesis 2:1-3, part deux

The second time I watched The Passion of the Christ, I knew what was coming, and I was ready. I was going to get through it without being totally destabilized, without gasping for air like a goldfish flopping on a theater seat. I wasn't going to get sucker punched again.

Emotionally I braced myself into my seat that evening, promising myself I would maintain my equilibrium and not get swept away by the gore, the horror, the violence of it. And I did pretty well until the moment when Jesus is carrying his cross down the Via Dolorosa and he stumbles. His mother runs to him and he looks her full in the face, one eye swollen shut and blood oozing from each thorn in his crown and says, "Look, mother, I make all things new!"

I lost it.

You might think it strange that this moment threw me so hard. I think there are a couple reasons. First, in the middle of my strapped-in, hunkered-down spiritual attitude, God caught me (once again) by surprise. And second, this is what the crucifixion is all about. It ties in directly, do-not-pass-Go-or-collect-$200, to this part of the creation story.

God says, "It is finished" here on the seventh day. He surveys all he has made and it's good. He's done a good job of creating, and now like any parent he's eager to see what this creation will become. Trouble is, creation gets broken and a deadly infection seeps in. What was good and whole and beautiful now writhes in wretchedness and pain. So God enacts his plan to re-create creation, to make it whole again. To make it new. The plan hinges not on a flood that will erase everything and allow a clean slate, but on God himself entering creation, submitting himself to the infection. He will fight it from the inside out. His end goal, though, is still the same: to make all things new. The crucifixion of Jesus is not just about erasing the hash marks on some cosmic demerit board so that you can escape hell. It is about all creation being healed and made whole again. You and I are a part of this, but it's bigger than we are. If you doubt this, read Romans 8 a few times. That will expand your thinking.

On the seventh day God finished his creation. On the cross Jesus says, "It is finished." In Revelation 21 God says, "Behold! I am making all things new." This thread runs from start to finish through the Bible. God so loved his creation that he gave his Son, so that the creation itself might be renewed, restored, healed, made whole. Right now it is happening here and there, now and then. This renewing of creation is partial at best. But someday God will complete the work and make a new heavens and a new earth. Peter describes this new heavens and new earth as a land in which righteousness is at home. (See 2 Peter 3.)

That new creation, and our place in it, hinges on the cross, where God defined the bedrock foundation on which the universe is built: self-sacrificing love. Where God reigns supreme, this self-sacrificing love flows through every molecule of creation, every relationship, every conversation. When Jesus described the kingdom of God to his followers, it was this foundation of love he was describing.

It was this self-sacrificing love that prompted God to create in the first place. This love moved Jesus to the cross. This love will someday make all creation new.

Transition: Genesis 2:4b and beyond

In the winter of 1988 I was desperately trying to escape from college. I needed a few extra transfer credits to make that happen, and to get the transfer credits I needed to talk my way into a religion minor. The transfer credits hinged on whether or not I could get the approval of John Helgeland, the head of the religion department. He knew I had been to a Bible college, but he wasn't impressed by that. He didn't have much time for piety of any kind, and he assumed the college I'd attended was all about devotions and not much for academics.

I sat in his office and he proceeded to give me a one-question oral exam that he figured would determine the extent of my academic biblical knowledge. "What are J, E, P, and D?" he asked.

Genesis 2:4 is a watershed in the creation story. According to some analysts, Genesis 1:1-2:4a is one version of the creation story, probably formulated by priests in ancient Israel. God is remote in this story, reigning over the heavens and the earth from a distance. The "second" creation story, according to this way of thinking, is the one that starts in Genesis 2:4b and continues through Genesis 3 and beyond. This story, according to this logic, is from a source that is older and tends to make God seem more accessible, more human-like, so God can come walking through the garden in the cool of the day. According to this view, these two stories came from different sources and were woven together later by a "redactor" or editor.

Scholars call this way of thinking the "documentary hypothesis." It sees various strands of source material (conveniently labeled J, E, P, and D) woven together throughout the first five books of the Bible. So if you sit in on some seminary classes or university religion classes that deal with these books, you will hear comments about the Priestly source (P), or the Elohist (E) or the Jahwist (J) or the Deutoronomic (D). The Jahwist and Elohist are named for the word they usually use for God; the priestly source is very orderly and includes many of the laws and genealogies. The D source includes most of the book of Deuteronomy along with a few other snippets.

For all I know, the documentary hypothesis people have it right and that is an accurate way to think about how the first books of the Bible were compiled. But the net effect of focusing on all this is that we start to position ourselves above the text and analyze why this writer or that writer might have thought such-and-such. We don't look at this so much as God's word anymore, but rather as the Jahwist writer's word, or the point of view of the Priestly source, and so on. We get infatuated with our own analysis of the text rather than letting the text stand over us and tell us how things are.

I passed John Helgeland's test, and got the transfer credits and my religion minor. I did indeed escape from college in the spring of '88. Whew. Almost a decade later I sat in another class, this time at seminary, in Terry Fretheim's class on the first five books of the Bible. A student asked a question about some uncomfortable part of the story, asking if that wasn't simply the Jahwist's anthropomorphic view of God, and we didn't need to take it all that seriously. I was so impressed with Dr. Fretheim's response. "Well, wherever that story comes from, it's in the Bible, and we have to deal with it." He was willing to stand under the text, to submit to it, to recognize it as scripture.

Whatever the sources behind the Bible's text, at this point the creation story changes gears. We will continue to read it as a narrative that tells us what is true here and now, not so much a

story about historical events. This is one way to stand under
the story, and hopefully to begin to understand it. It's the story
of you, and me, and who we are created to be and where we
find ourselves today.

Dust: Genesis 2:7

"The Lord God formed the man from the dust…"

I had a Kirby Vacuum Cleaner salesman in my living room once. He demonstrated to me over and over again how his beautiful vacuum cleaning system captured so much more dust and dirt than my pathetic old relic. He told me horror stories of how much dust inhabits the average home, of the chemical composition of your average dust sample, and how most household dust is actually human skin tissue. With science, with emotion, with fear he tried and tried to get me to spend the price of a good used car on his beautiful vacuum cleaning system. Strangely, though, the longer he talked the more I felt a sort of kinship with the dust in my house, a sense that I didn't want to get rid of it all. At least, not enough to spend $1500 on his metal-framed high-horsepower suction machine. Besides, I wondered what else might get eliminated by this powerful tool. *"Honey, have you seen the cat?"*

We come from the dirt, and if we're honest we never get very far from the ground. *Humus*, that's what it is, that dark stuff that makes the plants grow so well, and so we are *human*, and at our earthy best we enjoy a good sense of *humor*, and it's all interconnected. From the Pope down to the paupers, we have this in common. "Dust you are, and to dust you shall return," the priest says on Ash Wednesday to the hobbling old and to the bright eyed teenagers and to the baby in her mother's arms. He places a cross of ashes on their foreheads, the symbol of death, the symbol of new life in Jesus Christ. As much as we would like to deny it, this is who we are: we are fragile. Psalm 103 is a comfort here; it says that God knows us, and remembers that we are dust. You may expect yourself to be strong, infallible, to soar without error above your humble beginnings. But God knows you better than that, and in love he remembers the dust you come from.

We invent so many ways to try to get past our origins. Even Jesus struggled with his origins when he went home, reading the scripture in the synagogue (see Luke 4) as the patriarchs and matriarchs of Nazareth smiled and patted him on the head and said, *"What a nice boy! Why, I remember when he was just this big, Mary!"*

Is it any wonder so many kids from small towns can't wait to shrug out of the graduation gown and leave home? Many never really go home again. It pains us to go back to the source of our humility. We'd rather live with our illusions. There are still middle-aged men (they look strangely like the fathers of my classmates) in my home town who call me "Clenchy," the tooth-gnashing nickname of my childhood, though they've forgotten why they call me that and they mean nothing but good by it. After this many years away, the nicknames lose much of their sting. So I exercise the grin-lines around my middle-aged eyes and slap them on the back and recall some embarrassing story about our mutual childhoods, and we have a good laugh, remembering.

It's good to go home, back to the earth. Back to the place where I'm Art and Pearl's third son, back to Faaberg Lutheran Church's cemetery where the bones of my parents and their parents and their parents lie, going back to the dust from which they came. The day before my mother's funeral, my father and I walked out in the cemetery so I could see the plot he'd chosen for her, and eventually for him as well. We looked at the view across the fields to the home they had shared for thirty-five years, looked at the row of stately pines planted around the perimeter of the cemetery as though to keep the dead from wandering off. We looked at the headstones close by. I recognized many of the names. Dad glanced down at the one nearest to Mom's fresh grave. "Well," he said,

"Schroeders will be good neighbors." He'd lived his whole
life with his hands in the soil, and the thought of going back to
the dirt was not a fearful thing.

I walk out in the north pasture sometimes when I'm home,
down in the far corner. The summer I was eleven Dad and I
dug a deep hole into the dirt there to set a corner post. That
sweaty afternoon is one of the best memories of my childhood.
I look at that post now, leaning into the loose tension of the
wires, old and weather-beaten, half-rotten and slowly going
back into the soil, and I think about the dust I will someday
become. Ashes to ashes, and I will return to the earth. It's
incentive to live now with a sense of dependence. A sense of
finiteness, of the limits around my life. A sense of humor.

The Breath of Life: Genesis 2:4-7

God breathed into his nostrils the breath of life, and the man became a living being (see Genesis 2:4-7).

Most of us read this verse sort of like watching Dr. Frankenstein and his monster. The lightning flashes. God raises his fists in the air and exults, "It's alive!" Gabriel is hunched there doing his best Igor imitation while the man, who a moment before was dead as dust, stirs on the slab and sits up. Hmmm. Maybe our imaginations need some help.

If we gloss over this, the next couple chapters, or for that matter, the rest of the Bible, won't make a lot of sense. Remember that in Hebrew, the words for "breath" and "spirit" and "wind" are all the same word. So the man gets his lungs filled, but there's more than that. He receives God's Spirit. The breath of God. The old hymn has it right, I think:

> *Breathe on me, breath of God,*
> *Until my heart is pure,*
> *Until with Thee I will one will*
> *To do and to endure*
> *Breathe on me, breath of God,*
> *Blend all my soul with Thine,*
> *Until this earthly part of me*
> *Glows with Thy fire divine.*

This is the defining moment in human existence. This lump of dust is filled, infused, enlivened with the Spirit of God. This is the moment, the action, the presence, the quality that defines life. All the scientific debates in the abortion wars about when, exactly, life begins are dancing around the biblical point. In biblical terms life begins when the Spirit of God is poured into this lump of dust. With God's Spirit, we are alive. Without the Spirit, we are lost, dead, hopeless.

The other way we misunderstand this verse is we imagine some kind of divine CPR where God plugs Adam's muddy nostrils and makes a good seal and gives one quick breath, watching to see if Adam's chest rises... Adam coughs and sputters and begins to breathe on his own, and *voila!* He's alive! If life is about the presence of God's Spirit, Adam never does begin to breathe on his own. His life depends not on his own respiration, but on the Spirit. It's about God's presence in the heart more than it's about oxygen exchange.

Human beings have a deep, driving hunger for life. The genius of a Roman crucifixion was that it pitted a deadly, inescapable bondage against the human will to live. For hours, days sometimes, the crucified person without hope would push the weight of their body up against the spike driven through their feet to take the weight and strain off their diaphragm, to exhale, to draw one more painful breath rather than relax and surrender. Time and again we are amazed at what humans can endure in the quest to survive.

But this is not about surviving, as though a ventilator in the intensive care unit could maintain life. It is about living. There's a difference, and we too often surrender the ground between the two. I like the slogan on the commercials for Bear Grylls' show, "Man vs. Wild." "Bear doesn't just show us how to survive. He teaches us how to live." (By the way, did you know that Bear came to know Jesus through Alpha, and is now a strong advocate for the Alpha course?)

In my teens I pondered off and on why God says to the man and the woman that if they disobey him and eat of the tree of the knowledge of good and evil, they will die. More than that, God very specifically says they will die *that day*. But they go on for years and years, having kids and grandkids and great grandkids. Did God lie?

No. From God's perspective, the moment they turned from trusting him to trusting their own decision-making abilities, they lost his Spirit. They lost their reliance on his presence. Life, Spirit-driven abundant life as God designed it, ended in that moment. After that all Adam and Eve had was survival.

How many of us live in this day-to-day survival? All of us, I suspect. We mistake breathing for being truly alive.

What does it mean if "being alive" actually means being filled, animated, empowered by the presence of God in us, and without that presence we are effectively dead? What if, like in "The Matrix," the hordes of people walking down the sidewalk each day are not really alive, as God defines life?

This might have some implications for how we read the Bible, even how we understand Jesus. If this is the case, and if what Jesus said is true that he came so we might have abundant life (John 10), then the whole push of the biblical story from Genesis 3 onward is a drive not only to the cross and the empty tomb, but it is a push to Pentecost. Pentecost is that moment in Acts 2, after Jesus is raised from the dead, when God pours out his Spirit into this little group of fearful Jesus-followers and transforms them. He gives them life.

God is laser-focused not just on getting our sin-slates wiped clean, but on placing his Spirit in us, making his home in us, living within us, giving us *life*.

Eternal life is not so much about how long it lasts, but about how alive it is. It is not "ever-lasting life" so much as it is "the life that carries the qualities of eternity, the life God lives."

The question that begs asking is, of course, the most basic of all: are you alive?

True Masculinity

My daughter once had a scholarship interview with a university professor. She was asked, "What are a couple of issues that you feel are extremely important in the world today?" Her answers were first, society's tendency to see women as sexual objects, and second, the surrender of true masculinity. I think she's on to something. As we read Genesis 2, the Bible lays out a thought-provoking sense of what it means to be male and female.

In Genesis 1, God creates male and female together. There's a sense of balance, equality, and symmetry in this creation. And that is important, valuable, and true.

The Genesis 2 story highlights the contrast, the complementarity between male and female. This perspective is not contradicting Genesis 1, but enhancing it. It is also important, valuable, and true. In Genesis 2, the man is created first. So let's take a look at the man.

Interesting that God creates him outside the garden. Did you notice that? John Eldredge makes a big deal about this in his book *Wild At Heart,* and rightly so. The man is created out in the wilderness, and then God *puts* him in the garden to till it and keep it. There are a couple things to notice here about men. First, there is something undomesticated, outside-the-garden in the male heart. And this is a God-given gift. Society has tried again and again to file the rough edges off men, and when we have done so we have put ourselves at risk. Collectively, we need the rough energy, the barbarian capabilities of men. We need this not only in times of overt conflict, but perhaps even more in the quiet times of life when all seems peaceful and we are tempted to become complacent.

There is a wildness to male assertiveness that stands in tension, not necessarily in conflict, with female strength.

There's a great deal more to be said about this, and we could go on at some length. For the moment, I strongly recommend the books *Wild At Heart* and *Captivating*, the first by John Eldredge and the second by John and his wife, Stasi. These two books take a personalized, thoughtful, biblical look at maleness and femaleness. They are easy to read but also highly thought-provoking. Or, if you're looking for something different, find a copy of *Where the Wild Things Are* (the children's book, not the movie.)

I'm not joking about this. I'm convinced that *Where the Wild Things Are* is a brilliant work that offers deep insight into what it means to grow up male. Read slowly. Examine the pictures. Ponder what it means to grow up male, how it puts you in tension with domesticated life, and how every man at some point needs to go away to where the wild things rumpus. For those of you reading this from a female perspective, think: what is there about undomesticated man that is good, valuable, and necessary? Too many women have been hurt by men who are immature and out of control; that is not what we're talking about. The question we need to grapple with is, how can male wildness be redeemed without necessarily being tamed?

Too often men allow themselves to be tranquilized, (literally, "made peaceful"). This tranquilization comes from society, from the expectations of women, or perhaps most damaging from their own mistaken sense of what is "right" and "mature" for a man. Worse yet, men rebel against these mistaken perceptions and fall into a Peter Pan existence where they refuse to grow to maturity and remain immature little boys. When this happens we all suffer.

Look at the church if you doubt this. There is a drought in churches today of authentic male leaders. Men who succeed in the church are generally either good politicians, telling people what they want to hear, or they are tranquil men who meekly serve without ever offending, even for the sake of truth. It is a rare and precious thing in the church today to find a man who will faithfully, lovingly follow Jesus and proclaim his word without compromise even in the face of conflict or hardship. If you know such a man, stay close and hang on for the ride.

In the last couple decades, this kind of man has more often than not walked away from the institutional church. Many are still deeply committed to Jesus. But the institution has been revealed as deeply flawed, and many men have counted the cost of staying, then walked away.

So often men, especially young fathers, reject the church because they perceive it as a place where the rule of "Be Nice" will be forced on them. So they avoid church and cling to their bass boat, tree stand, golf clubs, widescreen TV, football games and beer bottles and barbecue grills. As a consequence they find themselves living a life that feels full but is in reality tragically shallow. But bring men like this alongside an authentic, Christ-centered man who can lead them in the high-risk life of following Jesus, and they will be challenged to a whole new level of excitement that is a far cry from simply "being nice."

One of the most tragic lies men believe is that retirement is a time for them to become more tame than ever. I understand the value of well-earned rest, absolutely. But the pool of experience and talent and wisdom present in a group of retired guys is truly awesome. When such a group gets their hearts and their feet pointed the same direction, wow! I am reminded of Tennyson's poem in which he portrays the aging Ulysses, hero of the Trojan War and adventurer *par excellence*. If you are interested in an alternative for men who face retirement years, ponder this poem. If not, skip it:

It little profits that an idle king,
By this still hearth, among these barren crags,
Match'd with an aged wife, I mete and dole
Unequal laws unto a savage race,
That hoard, and sleep, and feed, and know not
me.
I cannot rest from travel; I will drink
Life to the lees. All times I have enjoy'd
Greatly, have suffer'd greatly, both with those
That loved me, and alone; on shore, and when
Thro' scudding drifts the rainy Hyades
Vext the dim sea. I am become a name;
For always roaming with a hungry heart
Much have I seen and known–cities of men
And manners, climates, councils, governments,
Myself not least, but honor'd of them all–
And drunk delight of battle with my peers,
Far on the ringing plains of windy Troy.
I am a part of all that I have met;
Yet all experience is an arch wherethro'
Gleams that untravell'd world whose margin
fades
For ever and for ever when I move.
How dull it is to pause, to make an end,
To rust unburnish'd, not to shine in use!
As tho' to breathe were life! Life piled on life
Were all too little, and of one to me
Little remains; but every hour is saved
From that eternal silence, something more,
A bringer of new things; and vile it were
For some three suns to store and hoard myself,
And this gray spirit yearning in desire
To follow knowledge like a sinking star,
Beyond the utmost bound of human thought.
This is my son, mine own Telemachus,
to whom I leave the sceptre and the isle–
Well-loved of me, discerning to fulfill

This labor, by slow prudence to make mild
A rugged people, and thro' soft degrees
Subdue them to the useful and the good.
Most blameless is he, centred in the sphere
Of common duties, decent not to fail
In offices of tenderness, and pay
Meet adoration to my household gods,
When I am gone. He works his work, I mine.
There lies the port; the vessel puffs her sail;
There gloom the dark, broad seas. My
mariners,
Souls that have toil'd, and wrought, and
thought with me—
That ever with a frolic welcome took
The thunder and the sunshine, and opposed
Free hearts, free foreheads—you and I are old;
Old age hath yet his honor and his toil.
Death closes all; but something ere the end,
Some work of noble note, may yet be done,
Not unbecoming men that strove with Gods.
The lights begin to twinkle from the rocks;
The long day wanes; the slow moon climbs; the
deep
Moans round with many voices. Come, my
friends.
'T is not too late to seek a newer world.
Push off, and sitting well in order smite
The sounding furrows; for my purpose holds
To sail beyond the sunset, and the baths
Of all the western stars, until I die.
It may be that the gulfs will wash us down;
It may be we shall touch the Happy Isles,
And see the great Achilles, whom we knew.
Tho' much is taken, much abides; and tho'
We are not now that strength which in old days
Moved earth and heaven, that which we are, we
are—

One equal temper of heroic hearts,
Made weak by time and fate, but strong in will
To strive, to seek, to find, and not to yield.

What is God's design for men? There's lots more to say. But it
certainly does NOT mean that we give up adrenaline or a
yearning for wild things.

Knowledge: Genesis 2:9

God puts two trees at the center of the garden: the tree of life, which makes sense if life is really about the presence of God's Spirit like we've seen before. But he also puts the tree of the knowledge of good and evil there, and then tells Adam not to mess with it, which is a little confusing to us.

We think that knowing good from evil is a good thing. Right? We call it "discernment." We teach it to our children. We expect it of ourselves. Someone who doesn't know good from evil is a little scary; we call such a person a psychopath. But if we read the text carefully, the mistake Eve makes in the next chapter is that she wants to do a good thing. She sees that the fruit of this tree is pleasing to the eye, that it is good for food, and that it makes you wise. (More on this later.) What could be wrong with that? What is the Bible getting at here?

There's a problem with our knowing good from evil. Fact is, we too often get it wrong. Our discernment is not trustworthy. We set out to know good from evil on our own, and we mistake the two. Worse, we put our own sense of good and evil, right and wrong, ahead of the command of God.

Dietrich Bonhoeffer, a German Lutheran pastor who was hanged by the Nazis in 1945, wrote about this problem in his book, *Ethics*. He never finished the book while he was alive, but after his death the notes were collected and published. (We talked briefly about this when we were talking about God's creation being "good" in Genesis 1.) Here's Bonhoeffer's take on this issue. Feel free to take some time to ponder this:

> Already in the possibility of the knowledge of
> good and evil Christian ethics discerns a falling

away from the origin. Man at his origin knows only one thing: God. It is only in the unity of his knowledge of God that he knows of other men, of things, and of himself. He knows all things only in God, and God in all things. The knowledge of good and evil shows that he is no longer at one with this origin.

In the knowledge of good and evil man does not understand himself in the reality of the destiny appointed in his origin, but rather in his own possibilities, his possibility of being good or evil. He knows himself now as something apart from God, outside God, and this means that he now knows only himself and no longer knows God at all; for he can know God only if he knows only God. The knowledge of good and evil is therefore separation from God. Only against God can man know good and evil.

But man cannot be rid of his origin. Instead of knowing himself in the origin of God, he must now know himself as an origin. He interprets himself according to his possibilities, his possibilities of being good or evil, and he therefore conceives himself to be the origin of good and evil. (From *Ethics*, pp. 17-18)

I have a confession to make. I have started to read this book at least twenty times, and never gotten beyond this quote. If we understood this concept, it would revolutionize the way we think about good and evil, about a relationship with God, and about what it means to follow Jesus.

We see the consequences of our misunderstanding in well-meaning people who "believe in Jesus," but they see Christianity as a structure for living a good, moral life. In their minds the gospel can be summarized, "Be nice." Functionally these people are no different than the guy who sat next to me on the airplane who, when he heard that I was a pastor, responded quickly, "I'm a pretty good person."

Morally and socially, these are both good people. One has given intellectual assent to the person of Jesus, but the belief has no power to change their life. The other sees himself as an outsider to Christianity, but is still caught up in its moral framework to the point that he feels defensive when confronted with a pastor. Neither of these people has a clue what it means to know Jesus or of the power he has to transform the life of his followers.

It is only when we know Jesus first, last, and only that we begin to experience the power of his transforming presence. In his book *Life Together*, Bonhoeffer asserts that for the follower of Jesus, all relationships are mediated by Jesus. That is, no matter how close our relationship, we receive only as much of each other as Jesus Christ desires for us to have. Even for Christian husbands and wives, parents and children, the relationship is mediated by Christ. If it is not, to the extent that they know each other apart from Christ, they are cut off from the fullness of life that Jesus desires for them. In essence, this is what it means when God declares from Mount Sinai, "You shall have no other gods before me." When Jesus is all we see, all we know, and we know all else through him, we begin to experience what it means not to know good and evil in ourselves. We receive life in all its abundance as Jesus leads, as Jesus gives.

This life is the edge of the knife, for we can fall off either side all too easily. On one hand we may mistake who Jesus is and substitute a mental or emotional idol of our own creation without ever truly knowing Jesus.

So some people substitute a social gospel (the idea that the main thing God wants is to care for the downtrodden) for the truth of Christ. They believe they receive all things through the need, the demand, that social structures should line up with their "gospel." This is a favorite error of liberal Christianity. We choose a particular social agenda du jour (advocacy for women, gays, the poor, transgender people, for whales, for the environment, whatever) because we believe it is "good" and we superimpose it on Jesus, and from that moment on we hear Jesus recommending our social agenda.

But this Jesus is an idol of our own creating.

The error of conservative churches on the other side of the knife's edge is not really any different; we just substitute a "personal relationship with Jesus Christ as my Lord and Savior" (we used to abbreviate it PRWJCAMLAS) for the social agenda. Our error is to believe that this personal relationship is my only concern and now that I'm saved, I have nothing to worry about except perhaps helping to save another individual here and there. I can take my fire-insurance policy and go back to my self-oriented life. Again, we have missed the real Jesus in favor of an idol of our own personal creation.

The danger here is tremendous. In both cases, we have substituted a societal agenda for Jesus. One agenda comes from the political left, the other from the inner-focused fringe of evangelicalism that leans politically right. We are not governed by Jesus and his words to us, but by our sense of what is right. Many times I have heard "good" church-attending people or even leaders confronted by a statement straight out of the mouth of Jesus in the gospels, who say "I don't think Jesus would ever say that." Sometimes we dress our prejudice up a little better than that, but once we make this shift away from an external understanding of who Jesus is, we

can justify any behavior, any prejudice, any judgment, because
we believe we're following Jesus.

So the self-focused PRWJCAMLAS Christian can read the
gospels over and over but never hear Jesus' heart for the poor,
the sick, the blind, the leper. They can advocate for deporting
immigrants because it's their political platform, not realizing
that all of the Bible demands that we welcome the foreigner
within our borders. All these policies get spiritualized beyond
any connection with Jesus.

Similarly, the social liberal Christian can read the gospels over
and over and like Nicodemus in John 3, they miss all Jesus'
words about being born again, born of the Spirit. These words
run off their hearts like water off a duck. They advocate for
inclusion of all people, but they never let Jesus speak a word
of judgment or make any demands, because that would
contradict their inclusive political platform.

External accountability is critical, because we are so capable
of deceiving ourselves. If we are simply left to make Jesus in
our own image, the gospel is no hope and no help. A friend of
mine is a master at equipping leaders for ministry. Early in
their discipling he turns them loose on the gospels,
recommending that they read all four in order to get to know
Jesus. "Then what?" they ask. "After that, read the gospels,"
he says, "And then read the gospels again." We need to know
Jesus for who he is, not for who we think he is. And knowing
Jesus as he is, we need to surrender more and more of our
lives to him. We need to surrender our relationships, beliefs,
spending, saving, entertainment, social action, rest, laziness,
parenting, driving, work, shopping, everything.

Otherwise, if we hang on to our right to decide for ourselves
what is good, all we have done is to eat from the Tree of the
Knowledge of Good and Evil, and we have missed God.

Why? More on Genesis 2:9

Why did God put the tree of the knowledge of good and evil in the garden?

It's an excellent question. I think this is typically the way we respond to these things. Why did God set it up that way? Why make it so that it's so easy for Adam and Eve to fail?

Here's where my interpretation of Genesis drives people a little nuts. Because I don't think this is a story about what happened back then. I think it's a story about what is happening now.

The fact that God places the tree of knowledge in the garden is descriptive of the present, not the past. The question to ask is, why did God place the tree of knowledge (so to speak) in *my* garden? Why is that option always there, where I can choose to rely on my own knowledge, my own choices, my own tendency to rely on myself? Because the garden of Eden is really about you and me and where we find ourselves. That tree is in the story because it's in our story. The tree is in the middle of the garden because it's in the middle of our lives.

Observe God's desires for relationship with his created humans (think: us). In turn, observe human rebellion against God's desires (think: us). We have to ask, What is God's desire for me? Why am I always fascinated by the other options besides obedience to God? Why do I choose to rely on myself?

That's why the tree stands there in the middle of the garden.

Rivers: Genesis 2:10-14

These verses bothered me for years. Rivers don't behave this way. You don't have four rivers rising from one source and dividing into separate headwaters. The rivers especially don't go from one spot to both Iraq (the Tigris and Euphrates) and Ethiopia (Cush, where the Gihon flowed). Doesn't work that way.

In dry country, rivers are life. I lived in western North Dakota (a climate in some ways similar to Israel) for five years, a mile from the banks of the Missouri River. Driving that mile you would see an amazing transition from brown, dry, rolling hills down through the coulees to the lush, green bottom land along the river. Water changes everything. Throughout the Bible, rivers symbolize the presence of God's Spirit, the overflowing life of God, the flow of energy and power and vivaciousness that makes things grow. (See John 7:37-39 for example.) But in real life, rivers flow from diverse sources, then come together. They do not start from a common source and then separate.

But the story is about us and about our situation, not about what was true back then. So dig deeper. The river rises in Eden, in the garden. The garden of Eden is not a paradise in the traditional sense of that word, where life is all play and our every desire is sated. No, Eden includes work. (More about this in a later section.) Eden is creation as it was designed to be. In Eden we are fully connected to the powerful presence of God without barriers. The man (and a bit later, the woman) are placed within that creation not as tyrants but as caretakers. The soil, the wildlife, the plants and the people all live under the lordship and majesty of the Lord God who delights in this creation and comes walking through the garden in the cool of the day.

Now we begin to approach the point. Out of this proper relationship with God (he is Lord and Master) and with his good creation (we are caretakers), the rivers flow into all the world to water it and nurture it and bring it life. Life flows from proper relationship with God.

We so often miss this. We think we must get our lives together, get the river flowing right, and then bring that goodness into our relationship with God. But outside of Eden we can't do it. First we must enter into Eden, into right relationship with God and with his creation. Then the river starts to flow. This is what we are created for. We can't manage our lives and then bring our carefully managed selves to God for his approval. Instead we bring our brokenness and our shortcomings to God and discover that we are welcomed into his presence. As we will see, this is only possible through Jesus Christ and what he did on the cross. Once we return to him just as we are, he begins to transform us and our other relationships, including our relationship to the rest of creation. (Yes, I know there's an angel outside the garden with a flaming sword to prevent us from returning. But you're jumping ahead of the story. We'll get there.) The river of life flows out of the garden into the world, not vice versa.

Near the end of the Bible, in Revelation 21-22, we find these images recast. Now the river of life flows from the throne of God out to water the city where God's people are gathered together. God himself is with them, and he wipes every tear from their eyes. The separated nations are united around the throne. The four living creatures, representing all animal life, are there as well. The tree of life grows along the river banks. (You'll notice the tree of the knowledge of good and evil is not mentioned, interestingly enough.) All creation is together in right relationship under the lordship and majesty of God and of the Lamb, and their life flows from the throne.

Okay, so that's all well and good. What difference does it make?

How about this one detail. Take this one tiny example and extrapolate it to all of life:

If we get this, all the millions spent on Superbowl ads could be given to some worthwhile cause. All the hours of brilliant creativity that went into filming and computer graphics and scripts and actors and animation and special effects could be directed to something that benefits the world. All the billions of dollars consumers will spend on these products and all the billions of hours watching and rewatching and debating about the value of these various commercials could be redirected. Why? Simple. Because living in Eden, we will not be tempted to believe the lie that if we buy these products, buy into the value of these ads, we will have life. We will know that our life comes from a right relationship with God.

Work: Genesis 2:15

Why do we so often think of paradise being a place where we don't have to work?

Maybe it's because so much of our work here and now is a "have to." We don't realize what a wonderful privilege it is to have meaningful work until our work is taken from us (we get laid off, fired, we retire, we get sick or disabled) and we are lost. Work is written into our bones and our souls. It is part of the image of God that we bear.

But work (as we'll see later on in Genesis 3) has become a curse as well. "I owe, I owe, so off to work I go" says the bumper sticker. So we get bitter and twisted about work and we begin to imagine heaven as a perpetual vacation. We have been taught by Tom & Jerry to picture ourselves lounging on a cloud, living a self-indulgent life where no pleasure is off limits and it's all about me and what I want. This becomes our idea of paradise.

Fact of the matter is, after a few days (or hours, for the more intelligent and in-touch among us) such a self-oriented life would become torture. (I can hear some of you thinking, "Let me try it and see...") We rarely acknowledge that it was our self-indulgence that got us into the state of "I owe, I owe..." in the first place.

Why do we think paradise is a state of being without work? The garden of Eden includes a great deal of work, some of it probably pretty difficult physical labor. But work is part of God's good plan.

Imagine an existence in which work was like this:

No futility. Work never has that sense of deep frustration filled with unsolvable problems, unworkable solutions, and incompatible conflicts. There is always a way forward in tasks and in problem solving.

No drudgery. Every task is meaningful because it fits into a larger whole that has real purpose.

No boredom. Imagine work that was a constant challenge to your abilities, but you were also learning and growing into more effective, more fruitful ways of working all the time. Wouldn't that be fun?

No personality politics. Work would be a community effort without all the nit-picky trying to keep people happy around their pet agendas, their defensive strongholds, and their unpleasant personal habits. (Oh and the same about yours too, by the way!)

No moral quandaries. Work would never put you in a place where you had to ask if, at some deep level, you are compromising yourself either by the work you are required to do or the tasks you take on or the means by which you complete those tasks.

No shirking, hiding, avoiding, sluffing off. You would never find yourself on Facebook when you're supposed to be focused on work. You would never have to deal with the guilt of giving less than a day's work for a day's wage. Work would involve a perfect blend of effort and rest so that it was a joy to pour yourself into a task, knowing that there would be well-earned down time coming soon.

Do you start to see what work in the garden of Eden is supposed to be like? Certainly work would still involve a little bit of frustration. One of the good gifts of work is that it brings us to the end of ourselves and reminds us of our total dependence on God. That is a Good Thing. So it's okay for work to present a problem that we can't solve now and then, that requires us to rely on another and ask for help. But this kind of work sounds too good to be true. That's because we are used to the accursed work that is mostly frustration and meaningless toil, what the author of Ecclesiastes called, "chasing after the wind."

No, in the dream of God for his good creation, work is a total gift. As we learn to live in a right relationship with God, we begin to rediscover work for what it is intended to be. I'm always impressed by the conversations I have with new Jesus-followers. One of the consistent questions they struggle with is the question of work. What should I be doing? I sense a call to a different kind of work. I long for a meaningful, kingdom-of-God work. How do I start? What training do I need? How do I move toward this vision without creating a train wreck along the way? These are the questions of people who have crossed from dark into light, from death and despair and meaninglessness into abundant life. Jesus has called them to come and follow, and part of that following involves their effort. They come at this new work with a zeal and a passion and an energy that is exciting and contagious.

It's enough to make you feel like you're in the garden of Eden. And you are.

Rules: Genesis 2:16-17

I was privileged to grow up with an amazing sports complex right outside my back door. Fifteen steps from the back door of my house were two football fields. Not one, but two. A custom-constructed baseball complex was a hundred yards to the south. A softball diamond stood to the east. Now, to the uninitiated eye, this sports complex looked like a yard with some trees and a wrap-around cow pasture with a few rocks scattered here and there. But my brothers and I had carefully surveyed the entire complex, setting down boundaries, yard markers, end zones, bases, and a few extras not usually known in professional sports. (When was the last time the Minnesota Twins outfielders had to deal with a thistle patch? When did you last see a shortstop calculate his dive not only to catch the ball, but also to avoid landing in a fresh cowpie? I've wondered for years why coaches don't implement these training tools, at least in camp, for additional challenge to their athletes and for the greater benefit of their sport.) When we first started playing football in the front yard, we carefully measured the dimensions of the yard. We calculated that, as we were 35% the size of professional football players, so our field was roughly 35% the size of a professional field. It was all carefully proportional. In the pasture to the south, we precisely marched off the limits and boundaries of our baseball diamond in a similar way.

Have you ever tried to play baseball or football without boundaries, without rules? How about pinochle or poker? The game rapidly becomes chaos if the rules no longer apply.

People often reject the Bible because they think it is a book of rules, a compendium of "thou-shalt-not" designed to frustrate our fun. First of all this betrays their lack of knowledge about the content of the Bible; second, it betrays a warped understanding of God; third, it probably says a great deal about what these people experienced from their parents and others in authority when they were growing up. It says nothing at all about the Bible.

God, as we have already seen, is about giving life to his creation. He creates separation so that light may be known from darkness, land from water, heaven from earth, male from female. He makes knowledge and relationship possible through these separations. Humans are invited into this creation to experience its richness and fullness as a way of experiencing the love of the creator God. God creates amazing diversity of life. He creates plants, fish, birds, animals in amazing splendor, and then invites humans to know all these things, and even to name them (we'll see that coming up soon). Do you see? *If science is the pursuit of knowledge about creation, God created this pursuit and blessed it.*

One kind of knowledge is off limits. This is not placed by God in an arbitrary way ("Oh, I think I'll put the fence here") but in a logical, sensible, inescapable way. If we know God as the creator of the universe, as the origin and source of all life, as the lover of creation who has designed its intricacies and longs for its fulfillment, then we cannot know what is good for creation (including ourselves) apart from knowing God. If we want to know good, we must know God. If we try to know good apart from knowing God, we are treating ourselves as the origin and the source, and we will be deceived.

The boundary around the tree of the knowledge of good and evil is not arbitrary; it is part of the fabric of the nature of God and of the universe. God does not put this tree in the garden as a source of temptation; rather, his respect for and delight in the dignity of humans requires this possibility. If we do not have the option of seeking knowledge in ourselves, we are automatons without any possibility of growth or fulfillment.

But God knows, and we would do well to learn, that our deepest knowledge, our fullest joy, our most abundant life comes from an intimate relationship with God.

Jesus himself defined "eternal life" as knowing God (see John 17). Many languages have two words that mean "to know." In German, for example, *wissen* means to know a fact. But if you want to talk about knowing a person, the verb is *kennen*. We get confused in English because we talk about knowing God and knowing about God with the same verb. It's confusing.

Biblically speaking, the key is knowing God. It's about relationship.

In knowing God we delight to know his creation (including ourselves). So all the sciences are at their best when they seek to discover the truth about God's good creation. This is true for geology, biology, psychology, mathematics, medicine, both applied and pure sciences. Even Einstein said, "I want to know the thoughts of God." Charles Darwin, who early in his life received training in what was then called "Natural Theology," in the conclusion of his *On the Origin of Species*, implies (though he does not directly argue) that his theory of evolution provides the *mechanism* by which God's original creation has grown in diversity and grandeur. Study the history of science and you'll find that most of the great pioneers in the sciences were devout Christians.

We don't have to travel far to find examples of humans deciding for ourselves what is "good" and jumping wholeheartedly into it. Then we discover some time later that what we believed was salvation turned out to be dangerous and destructive. Asbestos, DDT, and Crisco have all been hailed as the next great development to enhance human life. Each one proved destructive and costly and we continue to pay the price.

These are relatively trivial examples; if we look at the way we destroy ourselves in relationships by doing what we think is right, we'll see in a hurry that we desperately need to submit to a loving God who knows us better than we know ourselves.

I thought God was a liar.

We touched on this before, but it's worth revisiting:

I didn't know how else to make sense of it. God says to Adam, making sure that he knows not to eat from the tree of the knowledge of good and evil, "in the day that you eat of it you shall surely die." (See Genesis 2:15-17)

But as the story goes on, we see that Adam and Eve do eat from this fruit and they live long lives and have many kids. So what's with that? I thought God was using hyperbole, overemphasizing the point to warn them. Maybe it would have just taken too long for God to say, "In the day that you eat of it you shall set forces in motion that shall cause the physical cessation of your body's functions someday years down the line." But that has to be what he meant.

Doesn't it?

Sometimes in the Minnesota winter I struggle with a nasty funk. Colds come and go, but a good funk is the gift that keeps on giving. I wake up crabby, snapping at people, resenting everything from my dog on up. Even I don't want to live or work with me, and I can't imagine what it's been like for other people who are stuck with me. Of course, being brought up as a Good Lutheran Boy I don't let my funk show in public if I can help it, and I still take out the garbage when I remember. But it seems I forget more and more often when my mind is in the hamster wheel of this funk.

The other day I was praying about some of this funk, trying to figure out why I've been strangling in its grip for so many months. I am not prone to seasonal affective disorder, so that's not it. Physically I have been pretty healthy, overall. But emotionally and spiritually I have felt like a little brown lump of infected beetle dung most of the winter. So when I got tired enough of all this, I started praying about this in more than the short, frustrated prayers ("throwing darts at God") that have become my practice. I started spending time reading my Bible rather than reading a verse here and a verse there and putting it off as long as possible. I picked up a book about growing in your relationship with God.

And almost immediately (say within four or five days, which after a three month funk is pretty immediate) I was diagnosed. I had turned my eyes from the truth of who God is and what God says about me to my own ideas. Simple as that. I had believed the lies of my own desires.

I was dying.

In my journal a couple days ago I recorded the quote that finally diagnosed me. It is from a book called *Conformed To His Image* by Kenneth Boa. Here's the quote:

> It is only natural to shape our self-image by the
> attitudes and opinions of our parents, our peer
> groups, and our society. None of us are immune
> to the distorting effects of performance-based
> acceptance, and we can falsely conclude that
> we are worthless or that we must try to earn
> God's acceptance. Only when we define
> ourselves by the truths of the Word rather than
> the thinking and experiences of the world can
> we discover our deepest identity… Loving
> ourselves correctly means seeing ourselves as
> God sees us. This will never happen
> automatically, because the scriptural vision of
> human depravity and dignity is countercultural.
> To genuinely believe and embrace the reality of
> who we have become as a result of our faith in

Christ requires consistent discipline and
exposure to the Word of God. It also requires a
context of fellowship and encouragement in a
community of like-minded believers. Without
these, the visible will overcome the invisible,
and our understanding of the truth will
gradually slip through our fingers.

When I set out to define myself, to create a truth about myself
apart from the will of God, I am cut off from the source of my
life. It may take me three months to figure out what's wrong,
but immediately I am dying.

This should come as no surprise; we've spent a great deal of
time already in Genesis realizing that being connected to God
is life. So, to pursue my own knowledge of my identity is
unlife, is death. In the day that Adam and Eve ate from the tree
(in the day I eat from the tree) the consequences are
immediate. God has not lied; I have simply failed to
understand and believe the truth.

So what about my funk? I'm retraining my mind these days
(see Romans 12:1-2) to remember that it is what God says
about me that counts. If I make plans or set priorities that are
not based on who God says I am, I crumple them up and throw
them away as soon as I realize it. When I find myself thinking
about myself or about others in a way that buys into a lie, I
consciously turn my mind away from the lie and remember
what God has said.

The crux of my problem this winter has been ambition. I have
wanted to be more, do more, achieve more, than what I have
been doing. Ambition is fine; but along with the desire to
grow I have swallowed the lie that if I achieve more I will be
more significant, my life will be worth more, I will make a
bigger splash in the world and somehow I will be greater. I
have forgotten who God says I am. I have bought into the lie

that I can market myself. I have chosen to focus on my own vision of what I might become and I have set aside Jesus' words, "I no longer call you a servant, but my friend." What greater status, what greater achievement, could I desire?

A field trip to Isaiah and beyond

We've figured out that when God says Adam and Eve will die in the moment they eat from the tree of the knowledge of good and evil, what he's saying is that when they turn their focus from him and try to live life apart from him, they will lose the only life that matters. Okay.

Let's turn it around. Let's look at what it means to accept what God says about me. Who does he say I am? Who does he want me to be? What happens if I let God define good and evil for me? Not only good and evil out there. What if I let God define what is good and evil in my own life?

This means letting God decide the direction my life should go. This means looking to him for my sense of myself. Every time I find myself starting to get ambitious (meaning, starting to get riled up to do something with myself that is outside God's intention for me, something that is designed to improve my image or my ability so I feel better about myself) I turn away from it and turn back to what God says about me.

One way to try this is to park in the last few chapters of Isaiah. Isaiah 40-66 is a remarkable piece of the Bible that resonates with the first few chapters of Genesis. Read through these twenty-some chapters and pay attention to what God says is true about you. It's huge. More importantly pay attention to what is true about him. He is the creator. He is the one who makes plans and makes them happen.

One of the things that always amazes me about Isaiah 40-66 is how much emphasis there is on God as the creator. Over and over again God proclaims himself the creator or Isaiah extols him as the creator or one or the other of them lays down the distinction between God, the true creator, and idols, who are pretty much created by a craftsman. There's a lot of responsibility that gets laid at God's feet (see Isaiah 47, for instance).

One example. Read Isaiah 51. Let yourself be blown away by the way God wants to re-create us when we are damaged, worn down, beat up, sin-stressed, or otherwise hurt. Take a look at verse 3, for example:

> The LORD will surely comfort Zion
> and will look with compassion on all her ruins;
> he will make her deserts like Eden,
> her wastelands like the garden of the LORD.
> Joy and gladness will be found in her,
> thanksgiving and the sound of singing.

God is speaking here to people who have lost everything, and he says that in their desert, in their barrenness, he will create anew the garden of Eden. He's using Genesis the way we've been using Genesis. He's saying, "It's your story. I'm going to create you anew, and just like the world was fresh and clean and verdant and glorious, so will you be."

If this is you, can you see what God wants to do?

When the later parts of the Bible use the creation accounts in Genesis, usually this is the way it happens. The rest of the Bible doesn't say, "Oh, look, God created everything so evolution didn't really happen." Equally, the rest of the Bible doesn't say, "The days in Genesis chapter one were actually about a billion years apiece, so there was plenty of time for the dinosaurs and all that carbon to get deposited." Instead, the Bible uses the creation accounts to tell you who God is and who you are. These stories offer hope because God is still creating, even in your chaos. Even if you're a refugee sitting by the bank of a river in a foreign land and your home country is lying in ruins, God is still creating good in your life.

That's the point of Isaiah 40-66.

Later in the Bible, John's gospel is a reprise of Genesis 1-3. The opening verses of John's gospel are a clear allusion to Genesis 1:1 and following. Then John shows us Jesus as the New Adam, walking through a broken creation and doing the will of his Father. Sin breaks in and has its way with Jesus and he is crucified. But this is not a defeat for him. Rather, he is returning to the garden of Eden and defeating sin, death, and hell. So when he rises from the dead "on the first day of the week," John is saying that creation has been made new. Just in case we miss it, John repeats that key phrase again. "On the first day of the week…" Mary Magdalene meets Jesus in the garden. She is a witness to all Jesus has done. She brings his word to the disciples. Mary is Eve as she should have been. When Jesus sees his disciples in the upper room, he breathes on them and gives them his Spirit, breathing new life into them. He is giving them life again.

It's Genesis 1-3 redeemed and made new. And Paul, in Romans 5, says that we who have received the free gift of righteousness in Jesus will exercise dominion as Adam and Eve were meant to do.

Alone: Genesis 2:18

One of my favorite e. e. cummings poems goes like this:

l(a

le
af

fa
ll
s)oneliness

The poem is usually referred to by the title "loneliness" and it's worth pondering a bit to see all that cummings packs into this tiny little creation. I'm amazed by the emotion that he communicates in a number of different ways. I think cummings understood well what God says about you and me, "It is not good for the man to be alone."

There is a huge difference between solitude and loneliness. Jesus was a great advocate of solitude, and the rest of the Bible backs him up. "Be still and know that I am God," declares Psalm 46. Mark 1:35 tells us that "before daybreak the next morning, Jesus got up and went out to an isolated place to pray." Solitude is almost a requirement (at least sometimes) for a relationship with God.

But loneliness is different. While solitude can be abundantly full of the presence of God, loneliness is desperately empty. Solitude offers the opportunity for reflection; loneliness drives me to despair. When we seek out solitude, we give God room to work in us. Sitting quiet for a half hour in the mornings, reading my Bible and praying, and sometimes staring out my window at the pine trees, is a discipline of solitude for me. Leaving the radio off when I'm in the car is another that I practice from time to time. Do you have disciplines of solitude? God will honor these times with his presence.

Yet God can use loneliness also. There is an emptiness in loneliness that allows us to face our brokenness. Loneliness forces us to face our wounds, to face the reality of ourselves in a new way. One of the formative experiences of my life was in 1998 when I graduated from seminary. To celebrate I took three days alone in the Boundary Waters of northern Minnesota. I prepared and planned, rented a solo canoe and chose a route that looked pretty remote. I intentionally didn't bring a novel or any other time-fillers. I was so looking forward to the solitude.

After a hard day's paddle to my first campsite I settled in to enjoy the peace and quiet. And I was immediately uncomfortable. Nervous. Fidgety. The hours crept by. I got my fishing rod out. I paddled around the lake. I watched a moose. I tracked a bear. Another hour crept by. I began to face a hard truth: without something to do, I was nearly frantic. All the peace and quiet was stressing me out. The isolation I had longed for was killing me. I had to learn a difficult truth on that trip. I was not the man I thought I was. I had thought I was all about peace and quiet, that I loved solitude and that I was quite comfortable with myself.

Oops.

That trip became an enormous learning experience for me. It was not good for me to be alone. I began to see a lot of my drivenness didn't come from my class demands at seminary. My hectic schedule wasn't something being forced on me from outside. I filled my days because I was afraid to be quiet, afraid to be alone.

Ouch.

Those three days became a defining experience in my life. A few years ago I talked to a friend who spends a lot of solo time in the Boundary Waters and told him about that trip in '98. "You think three days is bad," he chuckled. "Five days is the real crazy time. If you can get past day five you're good up to about ten. But five is really tough."

A few years ago I tried it. I planned for solitude. I included some good activities like a novel and a journal and a route that required me to move from place to place. I planned that trip as a way to seek God. And I expected that some of it would be uncomfortable and lonely. It was. And that was okay, because God can use that to teach me as well.

I think guys especially struggle with this business of being alone. Most of us have so many walls up that it's easier sometimes to be alone, even if we are lonely. But we want to be alone on our own terms, and come back to rub shoulders with others when we're ready. I don't think this is necessarily a bad thing, but we need to give God access to our rhythms of together and alone. That way he can use all of it. He can use our solitude, loneliness, togetherness, and community to shape us and teach us.

At the risk of stereotyping, women tend to be hardwired more for relationships. So there are a lot of isolated men hiding behind their walls, involved with lonely women who wish for them to come back into the relationship. But too many men haven't figured out how to invite anyone inside the walls. Too many men have no idea how to not be alone, even with someone else. Even in a marriage, even in a room full of people, these men are alone. Some of them don't even know it. They think they're miserable because... well, just because. Have another beer and try not to think about it.

So we discover again that God knows what he's talking about. It is not good for the man to be alone. There are deep wells to explore in this, but it starts with facing our isolation and seeking God in the solitude.

Fixing our loneliness: Genesis 2:19-25

It is not good for the man to be alone, God said. So what's the solution? God brings around a truckload of animals and the man names them and they have fun hanging around and playing frisbee in the garden. But the man still doesn't have what he needs.

Why does God do this? Doesn't he *know* what the man needs?

Wait a minute. Remember. This is not about what happened back then, it's about what happens now. It's about you. It's about me. So this part of the story is incredibly helpful to me. When we go looking for the solution to our loneliness in some other place, we find that as good as these things are, they don't satisfy. So I might go looking for a solution on my treestand during deer season. Or out in a boat fishing. Or in reading a novel. Or binge-watching a series on TV. Where do YOU go looking for solutions apart from God? Fill in the blank.

When I have a few days at home to myself, at first I revel in grinding my way through a few escapist novels or movies with lots of suspense and explosives. But then I start wandering the house aimlessly and all the books and movies waiting for me look like loneliness and boredom waiting to happen. I've been around the block enough to realize that I don't need more of those things.

One huge danger for us is that sometimes we buy into other activities to fill our loneliness, or we let our appropriate appetites grow beyond their appropriate boundaries. So a man develops an escapist habit of reading or fishing or golfing or woodworking or just plain working. These are good activities within boundaries, but they are unhealthy when they are allowed to grow too dominant in our lives. Then there are activities that are unhealthy from the start, and they will take a lonely person and make an addict out of him. So he turns to pornography that for a few minutes makes him feel alive, or alcohol in quantities enough to dull his pain. He gets addicted to the adrenaline rush of online poker because he keeps thinking he's about to score big, or he whiles away the hours with the fictional courage of video games.

It's not good for the man to be alone.

So God creates a... well, let's see. This is a tough word to translate. So let's stick with the Hebrew for a minute, because in English we get messed up in a hurry. God creates an *ezer* for the man. Not exactly just "for the man" either, but to be with the man. Like peanut butter was created for jelly, or rubber rafts and whitewater rapids were made for each other.

What is an *ezer*? Most English translations say something like "helper". That works, sort of, as long as we don't think "assistant." I've often wished for an assistant; someone who could come along behind me and do all the detail work, so I could focus on high and lofty and non-messy things. More honestly, I've wanted an assistant so I wouldn't have to clean up after myself. God is not saying he will make an assistant for the man. In fact, if you take a look through the rest of the Bible, *ezer* does mean "helper." But the only other times it's used in the Bible is to refer to God as the helper, as in "God is a very present help in time of trouble" (see Psalm 46). So unless you're tripping through life thinking God is there to clean up after you (if that's the case we need to talk, seriously) you have to realize that an *ezer* in Genesis 2 is not a way for a man to get a little secretarial help.

When God says he wants to make a help perfect for the man it means a help perfectly suited for him. The King James says "a help meet for him." This is not coining a new term, "helpmeet" which means assistant. In the liturgy we used in church when I was a child there was a line that said, "It is truly meet, right, and salutary that we should at all times and in all places offer praise to you, O Lord …" *Meet* in this case is an older English word meaning perfectly suited to one's need. So God decides to make for the man one who will be a custom-made help, one who will be perfectly made for him to take away the ungoodness of his loneliness. All the other good things in creation fall short of what the man needs. Fish and birds and zebras and koala bears, even golden retrievers, don't quite fit. But this *ezer* will be the perfect partner, the perfect help, the perfect one who bears the nature of God for him in a way that pierces through his illusions and his isolation to reconnect him to God, to himself, and to her.

Do we have any concept of the gift men and women are supposed to be to each other? This is where it becomes so important to read God's word not for entertainment but so that we might understand who we are, why we exist, and how we must live.

Ribs: Genesis 2:21-24

As we move into this section about husbands and wives and God's intention for marriage, we have to work through these verses at the end of Genesis 2. So man is alone, and God sees the aloneness is not good, and God decides to do something about it.

How often do we see this story played out? There's a fairly decent guy who is maybe in his early 20's or maybe his early 30's or maybe his late 40's, it doesn't matter. But everyone around him aches because he's such a fairly decent guy and why doesn't he find a nice girl and settle down but he just keeps doing his own thing and it annoys them to no end. My dad was 38 before he got married to the little girl across the road who somewhere along the way grew up and became a rather remarkable young woman who got a hold on his heart and wouldn't let go. When he was a bachelor, he did a lot of hunting and fishing until nearly every housewife in the territory had given up trying to figure out who Art should marry. Then Pearl got him. (Good thing, too, for my sake, or I wouldn't be here!)

We know this story. The man likes to be alone a little too much, and everyone, maybe including him, can see it's too much of a good thing. Then into his loneliness walks a woman with a light in her eyes and a flip of her ponytail and his friends are suddenly wearing tuxes and pouring Rice Krispies into the defrost on his car. (Don't do it. You'll NEVER get them all out, and every October a few more will come fluttering out when you turn on the defrost for the first time. It's a pain.) And in the fairy tales, that's the happy ending.

But we also live in a world where we know that the story goes on, and all too often it is a sad, difficult story. She may have kissed prince charming, and he doesn't *look* like a frog anymore, but he still likes to eat flies when she's not looking.

When I was working full-time as a pastor I sat in my office with way too many couples who had tried on their own wisdom for month after month to make their marriage work. Trouble is, they didn't know what it's supposed to look like, so they kept fighting and making each other mad. So he stomps off to the garage to be alone, and she calls her mother in tears. It happens way too much.

We won't solve people's marriage problems right now. It's going to take a while to work through these verses, because there is a lot packed in here. But let's start with a rib.

Why does God take from Adam's ribs to make this woman? Why not a different bone, or maybe just another pile of dust? Why a rib? (Note: In Hebrew the word means something like "side," but in English, "rib" serves pretty well.)

First of all, the rib means that these two are intimately tied. When he wakes up and sees her, the man recognizes this right away: "This is bone of my bones and flesh of my flesh," he says, which is a rough Hebrew approximation of "WOW!" He recognizes that this goes beyond the bond he had with the golden retriever, as much fun as the frisbee game was. Here is someone who is custom made for him, in fact made from him, so that in a sense these two fit together. To separate them now will cause irreparable harm. It will be like letting an oak tree put roots down into your heart and then tearing it out, roots and all. It leaves you behind, but you're shredded.

Second thing the rib tells us is that there's a symmetry, an equality, to God's intended relationship between a man and a woman. She's not made from his head to tell him what to do or how to think. Male passivity has allowed and encouraged (and sometimes required) women to step into the role of directors and dictators, but that was never God's intention. It is not God's intention today that she should be domineering and he should be henpecked.

Neither was the woman made from his foot so that he could stomp all over her, grind her into the dirt, use her and put her away when he doesn't want her around, make jokes at her expense, beat up on her when he's feeling threatened and powerless, or play her emotions like a fish, reeling her in and rejecting her simply to reassure himself that he's got some power. She's created from his rib, which lies underneath his arm where it can be held close, and which lies over his heart. She belongs *with* him, nestled up against the seat of his will and emotion. (Yes, guys, you do have emotions. They're in the tool box next to the 9/16 socket. Go dig them out and tell her about them sometime.) The rib tells us a lot about what God desires for this relationship.

But there's more coming.

God's ideas about marriage, part 1

I read once that everything the Bible has to say about marriage is in Genesis 2:24-25. Anywhere else the Bible talks about marriage is just reinforcing or commenting on these verses. The more I live with these verses, the more convinced I am that it is true.

Anyone who brought marriage issues to me as a pastor knows that I refer to these verses a lot. Premarriage counseling, marriage troubles, my own issues (and there have been many) around marriage, all of these draw me back into Genesis 2:24-25. I haven't gotten anywhere near the bottom of this well yet.

Genesis 2:24 lists three things we must do if marriages are to be strong. (It says the man does these things, but it has been my experience that both husband and wife need to do these three things to build a strong marriage.) First is to leave father and mother. Second is to cleave to each other. Third is to become one flesh.

Leaving home is difficult. For some of us it's tough to physically leave. I left home at 17, getting on the Greyhound in Grand Forks, North Dakota, and getting off in Seattle. For a kid who had never been out of the upper Midwest before (does a family trip to Kansas in 7th grade count?) it was a terrible shock to my system. I tried to adjust to college that fall, but the homesickness nearly killed me. It was so bad that when a friend planned an October weekend road trip back to Minneapolis for his sister's wedding, I jumped at the chance to ride along. Understand, this is an 1800-mile trip. One way. We left school Thursday evening, drove straight through 27 hours. I was home for about 36 hours. Then I got back in that Ford

Courier and rode all the way to Seattle where we pulled in late Monday night. All that was a result of my homesickness. It was bad.

For some people, leaving home physically is a relief. Home has not been a good place for them. Maybe it's abuse issues or personality conflicts. Maybe there's just no love. They run from home at the first sign of an open door. But it is especially hard for these people to let go of home emotionally. "Home" is surrounded in their hearts with all sorts of vows that start out "I will NEVER …" So they hold home in their hearts with bonds of judgment and condemnation.

No matter why we hold onto home, we have to leave before we can cleave. We have to let go of the way Mom and / or Dad always did things. We have to undo the bonds that hold us to the home where we grew up or we cannot enter into a successful marriage.

If we are not willing to set aside what we learned at home and recognize that we might have to learn new habits, new methods, new expressions, we cannot love effectively. Your parents might have been fantastic people. You might deeply respect them. But you still have to leave home, especially emotionally, before you can build a successful marriage. The relationship patterns that stood between your parents won't necessarily work for you.

And because your parents weren't perfect, it's even more important. So maybe your parents divorced, or were never married in the first place. Maybe you never knew one or both of them. Whatever your story, there is always brokenness to deal with here. You have to leave home to learn to give yourself to someone else.

You can still learn valuable lessons. But you can't assume those issues will go away when it comes to building intimacy.

It's the same with every area of marriage. Financial management, child-rearing, home maintenance, household chores, Christmas traditions, vacation plans. All these need to be renegotiated. You have to leave home, and it happens in a thousand tiny ways.

Too often a young couple gets married and everyone who loves them feels the need to offer advice. Fact is, bride and groom need to have a holy bubble that only includes room for three: him, and her, and God. Nobody else should have access to that most holy place in a marriage. Others can be close by, but they cannot be there at the core, or this couple will never grow strong. They need to protect the holy space at the center of their relationship.

What this does is create space for a relationship that is safe for both man and woman. It keeps the inlaws, the grandparents, and everybody else out of the bubble the two of them create.

What goes on inside that bubble? Next chapter.

God's ideas about marriage, part 2

Genesis 2:24-25, three necessary steps toward a healthy marriage. We already covered the first one, leaving home. The second step is to cleave to one another. What is so hard about that? Couples who are anticipating marriage usually can't keep their hands off each other. They have NO problem clinging to each other.

Then why is it that a year later, or two years later, these same couples came in and sat at opposite ends of the couch in my office? Chilly silence. No eye contact. They obviously have some HUGE resentments going. What's with that?

Part of the problem, at least, is that these two have not fully understood what it is to "cleave" to each other. They went out into a world that actively opposes strong marriages, and they were poorly prepared. As soon as a couple says, "I do" there are forces trying to tear them apart. Other relationships get in the way. His family, her family, friends of all stripes, work, recreation, different goals, different spending habits, different recreation habits, different movie preferences, different ideas about who does what around the house... there are literally hundreds of subtle differences that can worm their way in between a couple and shred their marriage.

Worse yet, each of them brings a whole host of wounds, assumptions, and judgments that affect how they see marriage, what they expect from their spouse, and how they express and receive affection. These are internal factors that may or may not be visible to each of them. But they have a huge effect on the marriage.

Cleaving means that we create a bubble at the core of the marriage that is a safe zone. It is a secure core to the marriage, and only three people are allowed in the bubble: him, and her, and God. No one else is allowed inside. Kids, parents, siblings, friends, all belong in their appropriate relationships, but a strong marriage has a safe bubble at its core with only three occupants. Anything that threatens that safe place must be excluded from the core of the marriage. This includes habits. Maybe one day he learns that what he thought was playful joking is really painful sarcasm. It needs to stop, because it's threatening the bubble and hurting his wife. Maybe she sees that her spending on a few little items here and there is causing her husband tremendous tension when he sees the bills each month. Each one is willing to sacrifice these habits out of love. Each one brings their habits to death for the sake of the marriage.

The tricky part happens when he recognizes that he has not only habits he can see, but also wounds, assumptions, or judgments that are less visible. If these threaten his wife, he needs to bring them to God for healing. They are endangering the bubble at the core of his marriage. And he needs to let his wife know what's going on so that she's in on the process of his healing. In the same way, when she sees that there are things in her life that compromise her marriage or threaten the bubble at its core, she needs to bring those things to the cross so they might die. The old fashioned term for this is repentance. There is huge vulnerability in this. There's huge humility in going to your spouse and saying, "I need you to pray for me that I could get past this, because I see that it is hurting our marriage." But if they cannot exclude from their marriage everything that threatens its survival, it will begin to die. There is no room for self-protection in this bubble.

Vulnerability is difficult. If you've been wounded, especially in early childhood, it will be hard for you to admit your faults and bring your weakness to your spouse. It's tempting to put a coat of armor over your weak spots. Control, aggression, and manipulation are much easier than vulnerability. But they will destroy a marriage.

Cleaving is about two things: 1) Commitment and 2) Time. Each one brings a commitment to honor that safe bubble. Each one recognizes that the death of those old attitudes may take a long time. We are in this bubble, the three of us, for the long haul. We cleave to each other taking hold of the Bible's promise that "a person standing alone can be attacked and defeated, but two can stand back-to-back and conquer. Three are even better, for a triple-braided cord is not easily broken." (See Ecclesiastes 4:12.) Two alone are not enough. It takes him, and her, and God, all cleaving together, in that bubble of safety at the core of the marriage.

God's ideas about marriage, part 3

It's been said that there are three steps to a healthy marriage: leaving, cleaving, and weaving. Kind of a handy way to remember the essence of these verses. We've talked about leaving home, we've talked about husband and wife cleaving to each other, but what does the Bible mean when it talks about two becoming one flesh?

The first answer that often leaps to mind for many people is that this "becoming one" refers to the sexual relationship between husband and wife. True, and it's important to acknowledge that there is a deep understanding in the Bible that physical union between male and female produces a oneness that goes far beyond a momentary act. This is why "casual" sex is so terribly damaging. If we don't understand that this physical act produces deep spiritual and emotional bonds, we will damage ourselves very quickly. We take what God designed to be part of a lifelong relationship of intimacy and we make it as casual as sharing french fries. When God included a commandment about sexual purity in the Ten Commandments, he was letting us know that this is serious. You don't break the law of gravity without getting hurt. And if we treat sex casually we're going to destroy ourselves.

But "one flesh" refers to much more than just our sexual relationship. One of the best examples I've ever seen of a one-flesh marriage is a couple I know who have been married for many decades. Not many years, but many *decades*. So they've had a long time to get used to each other. Some couples survive in marriage that long by distancing themselves from each other, but not these two. They have shared joy and grief, work and play and everything all their lives. I watched the two of them making breakfast once when I stayed with them. They had a narrow space to work in the kitchen. They maintained a conversation with me while they worked. He was making orange juice, she was mixing pancake batter. I couldn't help but notice that while he went to the cupboard for a pitcher on his end of the kitchen, he also grabbed a mixing spoon from the drawer because he knew she would need it. When she retrieved eggs out of the fridge, she also got the frozen orange juice out of the freezer for him. Neither of them asked the other to do anything. They were just very aware of what the other was doing, and they functioned like one four-armed person. It was almost as if they shared a mind and a body. *Exactly.* (See 1 Corinthians 7:4 and Ephesians 5:21.) This relationship took time and commitment to create. This couple spent years watching out for each other, paying attention to each other's needs, and learning how to serve one another.

Let me go a little further out on a limb with this one-flesh idea. The Bible uses the word "flesh" in a couple different ways. Sometimes it just refers to the fact that our bodies are physical, like a T-bone steak is physical, but still very, very good. (See for example Hebrews 2:14 or 1 John 4:2.) Other times, though, that word "flesh" refers to our old spiritual nature, our sinful self that fights against God's Spirit. (See for example Romans 8:12-13.)

I wonder sometimes, is the Bible implying that husband and wife become, in a sense, one "flesh" so that his weaknesses, his sins, his rebellion against God become burdens his wife has to bear, and vice versa? This is a difficult thought and one that makes me uncomfortable, but I see its truth in action. If he carries unforgiveness around in his heart, it damages his wife, even if she is not part of the relationship where he is holding a grudge. How much more does it hurt her if he is refusing to forgive *her*! If she refuses to be vulnerable with him and keeps her heart locked up, her rigid woundedness becomes his burden.

When we have an area of our lives where we indulge our
rebellious flesh and refuse to let Jesus have authority over us,
husband and wife can cause each other some real problems.
The most common areas where we experience this might
include selfishness, unforgiveness, resentment, a need to
control or manipulate, fear and anxiety, arrogance... the list
goes on. We bear one another's burdens (Galatians 6:2) as well
as sharing one another's joys.

On a personal level, I've been part of a marriage that ended.
My sins and my ex-wife's sins both contributed to that
horrendous breakdown. We tried for many, many years to
make a difficult relationship work. Eventually it disintegrated.
There is plenty of room for blame if either of us wants to go
down that road. I am culpable. So is she.

I can look now at these verses and see what should have been,
and sadly wasn't. I spent six years post-divorce dealing with
my own issues and bringing my faults to God. When I
remarried, I went in with both eyes open, seeking to apply the
hard lessons I'd learned along the way.

This book is about Genesis. It's not designed to be a marriage
manual. But here in these few verses, God lays out such a
profound pattern for what a relationship between man and
woman, husband and wife, should be. It's worth paying
attention.

Naked: Genesis 2:25

I saw a t-shirt at a church retreat once. On the front was a picture of some large wooden tribal masks, carved into stoic expressions; on the back it said, "Take off your masks. Pray Naked!" When asked about these interesting shirts, the young people wearing them explained that their group had done a Bible study on Genesis 2:25, focusing on how God wants a relationship with us that is totally vulnerable, totally open. But because we are sinners, we constantly wear masks.

John Eldredge, in his book *Wild At Heart*, talks about a similar thing when he describes how most guys (and I daresay the same is true for women) are posers. We swagger and strut, we pretend to know something about things when we actually don't have a clue ("Yeah, I was pretty sure when I brought it in that it was the muffler belt. Yep.") and in reality we are just pretending. Not in a good way. We're wearing masks.

In contrast, Genesis lifts up nakedness without shame as our state when we know God and each other face to face without fear. It is only when sin enters the picture that we feel the need to cover ourselves, protect ourselves, pretend to be something we're not. If not for the presence of sin in the world, I wouldn't get nervous sitting with my back to a full restaurant.

In the same way, it is the presence of sin in this world, and my long-conditioned response to its presence, that teaches me to cover my heart. I've learned to build the walls, to don a mask so I won't be hurt by someone's rejection or disapproval or scorn.

Nakedness is the prerequisite for not only a relationship with God, but for marriage. It is no accident that this verse comes hard on the heels of God's prescription for marriage: leaving, cleaving, and weaving. They were naked, and they were not ashamed. Married life (which, by the way, Ephesians 5:21-33 treats as a picture, a cartoon version if you like, of Christ's relationship with his people) needs openness and vulnerability.

You've probably seen, like I have, couples that coexist. Maybe they have had their fill of conflict and they at some point draw boundaries and say, "We'll share space but we will not get beyond each other's walls." Maybe they never figured out how to be vulnerable with each other. I'm constantly amazed when I plan a funeral and the children, or even the spouse, have little idea what was in their family member's heart. Spiritual beliefs? Not a clue. Deep loves? Well, she enjoyed pinochle. What was important to him? He liked building birdfeeders. Any idea what he thought about God? We never talked about it. What did she believe in? Um, we don't really know.

We hide our hearts from each other not out of some noble stoicism, but out of fear of being hurt, plain and simple. We don't know how to be naked at a heart level.

And sometimes those who are most capable of being naked physically are the most guilty of hiding their hearts behind walls. Whether it's the free love of the 1960's or friendship with benefits of the 2000's, all we do by getting naked together is satisfy a temporary lust for affection. We completely miss the intimacy for which God created us.

What makes this kind of vulnerability possible? It's fairly simple. We cannot be forced into vulnerability. We must be loved into it. Love creates safety. Safety does not mean you will never experience pain; rather, it means that I will not selfishly hurt you. If you are in pain, I will come alongside you.

God loves us by seeking us out, coming alongside us, standing with us when we are in pain, and speaking no word of condemnation. By the time we see God coming alongside we have already been condemned amply and fully by the laws of the universe. (Yes, God made the universe that way, so yes they are his laws... but God doesn't run around like a referee in a striped shirt blowing his whistle when we make a mistake.) We don't need another word of condemnation, and God knows it. We are wounded enough already, wounded to death. So Jesus comes not to condemn (see John 3:17 or Romans 8:1) but to save. He comes to bring resurrection. Like the Samaritan in the story, he dresses our wounds, lifts us up and places us on his own donkey (Luke 10) and brings us to a place of safety.

This is God's model for love, and indeed God's model for marriage. This is how we are to care for each other. Not by condemning or manipulating, but by coming alongside one another and caring for each other. Tenderness matters.

We are wounded enough already. So if your chosen means of expressing affection is the sarcastic jibe, find a different way. Be vulnerable and give an honest compliment that might be rejected. Open your heart and speak your affection instead of offering a backhanded insult. That's a mask. Learn to get naked, even a little bit.

Time Out: Looking back for a moment

We've come to the end of Genesis 2. We're actually making progress. Slow, sometimes tedious progress, but I hope you're seeing a little of the depth that is possible digging into the Bible. We have not exhaustively covered Genesis 1-2. Not even close. There is no bottom to this ocean, and you can always dig deeper. There is so much more we could talk about.

There is a lot of uncovered ground in our romp through Genesis. At the end of Genesis 2, however, we can say a few things:

- Creation, whatever the methods God used to make it so, is the work of a loving, attentive God who is relational and personal and stays engaged.
- Creation is good. Many many times God says so. Notice that he doesn't say perfect. We sometimes get screwed up because we think Eden was a totally perfect system except for that free choice thing, and if God could only have found a way around that we'd all be happy robots singing praise and eating papaya fresh from the beautiful trees, but not that one tree, to this day. No, Genesis is clear that creation is a beautiful, good place but it has some dangerous parts as well.
- Creation is orderly. Chaos is the enemy of goodness, except where chaos becomes the raw material out of which God makes goodness. The goodness of creation demands basic order, including some distinction and separation. You are not me and I am not you. Boundaries.
- Humans are made for relationship. This theme perhaps more than any other (except the sovereignty of God) dominates Genesis 1-2. We read about being

created in the image of a relational God. We read
about our relationship to creation, and our task of
stewarding the earth. Then in chapter 2 we read about
the man's desperate need for companionship, his
appropriate relationship with the animals, and the
goodness of male and female relationship.

We could certainly say more. Lots more. But suffice it to say
for the moment that Genesis 1-2 provides a climb to great
altitude where we can peek into God's purpose for creation
and for us specifically. Now we have come to that point on the
roller coaster where we've reached the pinnacle and we're
about to plunge into the abyss. Genesis 3 is the watershed of
the whole Bible. Here we go.

Genesis 3: Brace yourself

In true Genesis form, we don't get any explanation where the snake comes from or why it's in the garden. For that matter, we don't get a reason why God put the tree of the knowledge of good and evil there either. It's just there.

Again, it seems like Genesis is not trying to give a cogent account of what happened in some past time. Or if this is a record of past events, it's offered with little thought for rooting the events in history. The point, whatever the historicity of this story, is mythological. Not at all in the sense that these things are false. Exactly the opposite.

To look at it differently for a moment: Why is the snake in the garden? Not because God is testing us, but because in your life and mine, there is a snake in our garden. If the narrative didn't include the snake (and the tree, for that matter), it would be totally unrealistic. It would not connect with our real lives.

Temptation is present, from a number of different sources. There are powers (including yourself) that are out to trip you up. It's just reality. It's helpful to see these verses as describing the realities of our life rather than saying we suffer today because God didn't set things up as well as he could have in some past time.

In that sense, this is a mythological story. It is true right here, right now, in the coffee shop where I'm writing. In fact, there are many parallels between this spot and the Garden of Eden. It's a good place. All my needs and some of my wants are supplied in this place, and I recognize that God has provided (through the work of some individuals) all this for me. I've had many a good conversation with God here, and I've also spent time here doing the work to which God calls me.

Writing, having conversations, praying, meeting new people, getting reacquainted with old friends. Yet there are opportunities here to step outside God's intentions for me as well. Most obvious is the cheese danish in the case up at the counter. But there are less obvious, more "crafty" (depending on your translation) temptations as well.

The most crafty temptation here is to lose touch with God and begin to experience life for myself. As Dietrich Bonhoeffer said, if I want to know God I can know only God, and all other things through God. As soon as I know anything apart from God I have lost the knowledge of God. So the cheese danish, the other customers, the owner, the coffee, the laptop, the sunrise, are all available to me in two distinct ways. I can receive them all as gifts from God to be received appropriately and used in obedience and love that springs from a strong connection to God as my source and my guide and my center. Or I can access each of these God-given gifts as things available to me directly, to be managed, used, or worshiped as I choose. This is the question for us in every moment, in every Eden where we find ourselves.

And there is a snake. I am not left on my own to gently reason these things out and come to a good decision about choices. No, the choices come at me hard and fast, crafty and subtle. Before I know it I have begun to consider the fruit in its own merits rather than knowing the maker of the fruit. Because you have to make the choices, don't you? Is it possible to opt out of the decision making of this life?

Probably not. But we can reduce the number of decisions, and we can certainly reduce the number of temptations. "In repentance and rest is your salvation, in quietness and trust is your strength, but you would have none of it," God said (see Isaiah 30). Truth is, we *like* making our own choices, and we *enjoy* the frantic pace of our lives. We choose these things again and again when God lays out opportunities for repentance and rest, quietness and trust.

So we find ourselves grateful for the snake, and we work in league with him for our own destruction. We need to get tired of eating from the fruit of this tree. When the knowledge of good and evil on our own terms has tied us up in knots time and again and we descend into slavery, we begin to yearn to be dependent on God, rooted and grounded in him and him alone. Until then we keep saying, "I'll just do this one on my own..." and the story happens all over again. It's our story. The coffee shop, the office, the living room is the garden. I am Eve. I am Adam.

The serpent's methods: Genesis 3:1-5

Have you noticed how the snake works? We see a pattern here which is so often replayed in our own temptations.

First, he gets us to doubt God's word, and to focus on the things God prohibits. So instead of seeing the entire garden of luscious fruit around us, we focus on the prohibition, the one tree God has placed off limits. God has spoken clearly to most of the issues we face. If we know God's word at all, the serpent's tactic is to get us to question or doubt it.

This is subtle most of the time. It's not like one day we face a decision and start to say, "The Bible is false!" No, it's more like this: I know God's word says that "in repentance and rest is my salvation," (Isaiah 30) but I feel the pressure of my to-do list, so I focus on the tasks I want to do rather than on the rest God provides. I think, "I'll rest tomorrow. Or maybe the day after. Today I have to get things done." So I doubt that God knows best, because if he saw all the things I'm responsible for, he would have written that verse differently, right? Or maybe I think to myself (and this is so very subtle) "Yes, God's word says I should rest; but it also says I should work hard, and you have to know how to apply the word." So I step back from the word that God's Spirit is speaking to my heart (the call to rest) and begin to debate with myself. Rather than simply accepting that word as the authority over my situation, I enter into a confusing debate that makes me pit some parts of God's word against others. Step one accomplished.

Second, the serpent denies the penalty for sin that is contained in God's word. "You will not surely die," he says, in direct contradiction of what God had said in Genesis 2. So in the above illustration, I start arguing with God's word. "My salvation doesn't depend on whether I rest or not," I tell

myself. Salvation is by grace, after all, and saying it's
dependent on rest is some wacky kind of works righteousness.
So I get to work on my to-do list. At this point I have
effectively listened to the voice in my head instead of God's
word. And the voice in my head says something which, while
theologically and biblically true ("salvation is by grace"), in
my particular context it directly contradicts the word God is
speaking to me. What I'm doing here is taking my debate a
step further. I'm moving to the level of consequences. "Yes, I
know I need rest. And it sure would be nice to take a break.
But I'm so busy, and I need to get this done. It won't
jeopardize my eternal salvation, after all."

What I don't realize is that my salvation in this sense is not
only about my eternal status, whether I will go to heaven or
not; it is a question of whether I will begin here and now to
experience the "abundant life" (John 10) that Jesus came to
give. So my theological correctness keeps me from
experiencing the fullness of all God wants for me here and
now. Step two accomplished.

Third, the serpent casts doubt on God's character. "God knows
that when you eat of it, you will be like God, knowing good
from evil." In other words, God isn't willing to share his
power, his knowledge, his God-ness. He's holding out on you.
How many of us somewhere along the way have bought into
the idea that God is something less than entirely good? He
messes with us, he holds out on answering our prayers, he
creates trouble in our lives for his own hidden purposes. He is
not trustworthy, he is not really good. While he doesn't give
me more than I can handle (who came up with that idea?) he
still dumps bad things into my life, or at least lets it hit me. We
have believed the snake over and over on this one. The issue is
not that we believe God allows evil to happen. The issue is
that deep down we believe God has something less than our
best interests at heart.

Playing out our illustration about rest, I deep-down believe that God has set me adrift in this difficult world. I have to work hard to get anything done. It's not like I can just sit back on my laurels and enjoy the benefits of life. I have to work.

Have you ever noticed how the most effective lies are 95% true?

Yes, it's true that hard work is important. But it is also true that God has called me to live in union with him so that when it's time to rest, I trust him fully and completely. Rest is about knowing peace in God's presence. My desperate need to stay busy is rooted in a conviction that God is not really good and abundant. He will not pour out the blessings of heaven for me. And if I choose to rest, I will lose out.

Step three accomplished.

Now the snake has inserted a wedge into my relationship with God. Rather than knowing only God and receiving all things through God, I'm dealing with the questions on my own. And in doing so, I have already walked away from the relationship with God that he desires, and for which I am created. Taking a bite of the forbidden fruit is only the consummation of a shift that began with me "thinking for myself."

That darn snake. Later the Bible, and theologians down through the ages, will associate the serpent with Satan. There are some powerful passages later in the Bible that draw this association out. Revelation 12 is one of the best. In some ways it's a reprise of Genesis. There's a woman, and a serpent, and a flood. And God is working out his plan to send a Messiah who will rule the nations. Another place in Revelation we hear that salvation, and power, and kingship, and authority have come to Jesus. He has reversed the dragon's takeover of creation.

The serpent is a theologian

Let's be clear about something as we read Genesis 3. The snake doesn't have any problem talking about God. Speculating about God, wondering about God, thinking about God. These things don't bother the serpent at all. Eve and the snake have a great theological conversation. In fact, it's the first theological conversation recorded in scripture. And if we pay attention, we might learn a really valuable lesson here. Namely:

Talking about God, being interested in God, even being fascinated with God and the things of God will not save you from wandering away from God.

Shouldn't this be obvious by now? How many great Christian leaders fall each day and we shake our heads because we are thoroughly jaded? As I write this, the Vatican is embroiled in the latest string of accusations and counter-accusations about who knew what about which priest was molesting which kids. These scandals and accusations and confessions have become far too common among Christian groups of every stripe. We have enough skeletons in our own closets, and so does every other group of Christians. This is not unique to Catholics, or Evangelicals, or Pentecostals. Every kind of Christian group has their scandals.

Thing is, we need to learn this simple truth. Talking about God is no defense against sin.

Think about this for a minute. Eve (and Adam, because he's standing right there, which we'll get to before long) has the option of, at any moment, crying out to God instead of speculating about him. Can you imagine how different the story would be if Eve said, "Lord, what do you think of what this scaly critter is telling me?" Speaking *to* God, as opposed to speaking *about* God, short-circuits temptation more often than not.

Here's an illustration. The classic temptation for men is lust, right? In the spring when the weather warms up, there's a particular scenario that plays out all too often. Joe Christian is minding his own business, driving down the boulevard, and there's a beautiful female jogger. She's wearing considerably less than she was when he saw her jogging two months ago. Joe's thoughts rush down channels that are pretty seriously unhealthy. He spirals into a chaotic mess of fascination and shame. He looks, and looks away, and looks. The image of her jogging and all that's associated gets seared into his brain.

To be clear, she's just out for a jog, taking good care of her body. The issue is all in Joe's head. It has nothing to do with her.

So what do you do with that kind of temptation? Reading Genesis 3 creatively, here's a thought. When you recognize the temptation to let your thoughts go in unhealthy directions, pray for her. That woman you see jogging. Pray that she'll have a good run. That the runner's high she gets out of her workout draws her closer to God. That she has good relationships at home, whoever she lives with. That God would work in her life. Talk to God about the woman you see and she will no longer be a temptation for you, in your actions or your thoughts. Invite God into the conversation.

Ladies, I know you have your own areas of temptation but I'm confident you can translate. Talk to God about what tempts you.

Do you see how simple, but how radical, this is? If we talk to God, it invites his power and his presence into the temptation in our lives. It changes things. Doesn't fix 100% of everything, no, but it changes things in real ways. If we only agonize about temptation, if we simply wish it would go away, we're roasted.

But Eve (and the silent Adam) ignores the possibility of inviting God into the conversation. And she falls, and he falls, just like we do. Oh, yeah. Remember? It's *our* story.

What's the problem with the choice Eve makes?

We need to learn to read the Bible for what it says, not for what we think it says.

So when you read Genesis 3 and pay attention to the decision Eve makes, what's wrong? She notices three things about the fruit of this particular tree. First, it's good for food. Nutritious. Eve is reading the label. Totally organic. Part of a balanced diet. She's thinking about the good of her body and her family, and this is a good choice.

Second, the fruit is "a delight to the eyes" (ESV). It's beautiful. It's attractive. Eve, like most women, pays attention to her aesthetic sensibilities. She notices when things are out of harmony. She appreciates coordination and beauty. So the fruit is not only nutritious, it is attractive, it's beautiful, it's pleasing. Having this around her will enhance her home and her life.

Third, it is "to be desired to make one wise." Eve is not only thinking about food on the table and about visually pleasing surroundings. She is looking ahead, trying to improve herself.

So what's wrong with Eve's decision? She sounds like an informed consumer. She is making a responsible, ethical, good choice. How come the Bible, and generations ever since, have condemned this choice as evil? Even the Apostle Paul says she was "deceived" (see 2 Corinthians 11:3 and 1 Timothy 2:14) by the serpent. How so?

It's fairly simple, actually, and it's disturbing to the core for those of us who try to live good lives because we want to please God. Eve made a decision on her own. That's all there is to it.

Well, there is one tiny detail more: Eve made a decision on her own regarding something about which God had already given instructions.

So when someone comes to me and says, "I know the Bible says ___________, but I've been thinking this through and I believe doing this other thing is a better decision" I hear the echo of the serpent's voice.

For example, think about the many, many people who are stuck right now in financial hardship because they overextended themselves to get into a bigger house or a larger mortgage. They made good decisions based on what seemed wise and the good advice they were getting at the time from their mortgage broker. "I know the Bible says I shouldn't go farther into debt, but the housing market keeps going up and if I don't get in now, I'll never be able to afford this house..."

Or think about the many, many people who have overextended themselves by buying toys (plasma TV's, ski boats, second or third homes, timeshares...) who thought, "I know the Bible says to live a modest and quiet life, but you have to enjoy life a little, too, and I've earned this."

Or those who got in over their heads using credit cards, who thought, "I know the Bible says debt is foolish, but the Bible was written in ancient times, and this is the way things are today."

It's not only finances, either. Plenty of people have bailed out of marriages or given up the habit of regular worship because they think they know better. And they suffer the consequences. In the moment when we face those decisions, we're not trying to be disobedient. We're not trying to be bad people. We are hurting, or desperate, or frustrated. And we reach out to the one thing that looks like a good solution.

That's the thing. We always want to make up our own minds, make our own decisions, do what seems right to us, and we never want to live with the negative consequences of our actions. Just like Adam and Eve.

So biblically speaking, is there any such thing as a good decision? I don't think so. I think there are godly decisions and ungodly decisions. The only people who could possibly, in biblical terms, make a good decision are those who have never heard God's word and are trying their best to live wisely without the knowledge of God. (The Bible talks about this possibility. See Romans 2, for example.) The rest of us are accountable to seek God and make godly decisions. When we don't do this, we carry the consequences of our actions.

Of course, God's good promise is that he works. God works even in our foolish decisions, even in random evils that occur in the world, even in the face of systemic evil that overcomes us. He works to bring about good for our sake (see Romans 8:28). He is faithful, even when we are faithless.

Adam's culpability: Genesis 3:6

So what's with Adam? He'd be off the hook in this story except for four words, in English. Genesis says she gave the fruit to Adam "who was with her." Those four words place Adam's guilt front and center. You see, up till now it's all Eve. She's having the conversation, she's evaluating the options, she's choosing the fruit, she's making the decision, she gives some to Adam and sucks him into her fall from grace.

But Adam was there the whole time.

That's the problem, isn't it? Look at us. Who takes charge of passing on faith to a new generation? By and large, the women of the church do. Who takes charge of making sure dollars, time, and energy are given to feeding the hungry, helping the poor, clothing the naked? Mostly the women. Who drives the fellowship activities of the church? The women. Who leads music, with a few notable exceptions? Probably more women than men in most churches. Who is taking the role of spiritual leader in most church members' homes? Usually it's mom. Who sets out high expectations of moral, ethical behavior for children? Mom. Who encourages children to make worship a habit? Mom.

Where is Adam?

He's right there. He's standing there the whole time. Once in a while he'll even get into the spirit of things, with a hearty, "You need to listen to your mother." He spends Sunday morning watching television or going through his tackle box, and the kids know enough to watch his example rather than listen to his words.

Eve is having the most important conversation of humanity's life, and Adam is looking for the remote. Eve is making decisions that will affect her progeny down through the generations, and Adam says, "huh?"

Imagine if Adam took his role seriously. Imagine if Adam overheard part of the conversation between Eve and the snake and stepped up and said, "Honey, don't listen to Slither over there. Remember what God said? I know it looks good, but everything we have today we have because God gave it to us. We need to obey what he told us." Or better yet, Adam could turn to God. "Eve, we need to pray about this before we make a decision."

Most of the time Adam is either clueless or he's scared. (To be clear, by "Adam" I'm referring to me and other guys like me.) Plain and simple. Some of you guys read the last paragraph and the idea of praying out loud with your wife scared you to the bottom of your tennis shoes. Some of you are vaguely disturbed by the whole topic because you sort of think you're getting scolded for something you didn't do, and you're not sure what it's all about.

Spiritually passive men. Since time began this has been a huge problem for God's people. All through the Bible you can see this story repeat time and time again. And all through churches today. And all through your house and mine. Far too often it's the woman who drives the family spiritually, and when she suggests that the family attend worship together, the best she gets from her husband is, "Okay, if that's what you want." More often, she hears "That's fine for you, but I'm not going."

Adam just stands there. His family, his marriage, his relationship with God are all falling apart, and he stands there. And when his wife screws things up and offers him the fruit of disobedience, he takes it and starts munching. Later he'll blame her for his fall. It's not a pretty picture.

Is it any wonder so many of our heroes are men who have shaken off their passivity? Look at William Wallace in "Braveheart" or Maximus in "Gladiator" or Neo in "The Matrix" or any of dozens of others. These men have grabbed hold of the meaning of their lives with both hands. They still have questions, fears, and uncertainties but they are *acting* in the face of it all. They make mistakes, but they are scrambling to do the right things. You've got to respect guys like that, even when they fail.

The bad news is good

Reading Genesis 3 is hard. It can feel at times like we're
getting beat up, like we're more sinful than we thought, like
this is bad, bad, bad news. And it is.

But if you don't have an accurate diagnosis, the doctor can't
help you much. The deeper we dig into Genesis 3 (and by the
way, we have a looooong ways to go yet) the worse things
look. We find out that we are in bondage to sin, that we sin in
thought, in word, in deed, by what we have done and by what
we have left undone. We have not loved God with our whole
hearts. We have not loved our neighbors as ourselves. The list
goes on.

So how do we deal with this? Stop reading? Decide to read
something else? Get a second opinion?

God's desire is that our sin should finally have its way with us.
Strange as it sounds, God wants our sin to beat us down and
beat us up until we are willing to turn to him.

He is not mean or angry. He loves us. And so he is unwilling
for us to remain in bondage to our sin. Once we are beat up by
our sin and turn to God, everything changes. We come to the
cross of Jesus and there, hanging between heaven and earth,
we see the full measure of our sinfulness. We see that our sin
has earned us death. That we are thoroughly corrupt. And in
our corruption, while we were yet sinners, God did for us what
we could not do for ourselves. He came in Jesus of Nazareth
to live and die to rescue us from the deadly consequences of
our sin. He came to die and to rise, to conquer the death we
have earned, so that we might have his life. Not our own old
worm-eaten corrupt life, but the new, holy life he gives. As we

turn to him and to his cross, as we welcome the risen Jesus into our lives, he begins to live his life in us.

It's amazing to listen to the voices of those who have come to know Jesus in this way. I remember many times listening to the Teen Challenge choir when they would come to my church. These people who had suffered so much because of their sin and bondage sang their hearts out, telling how Jesus saved them from the death they deserved. When they sing, "my chains are gone, I've been set free," they know what they're talking about. Jesus has rescued them out of addiction, abuse, crime, homelessness, death of every kind. He is living his new life in them, a little more each day as their sinful past comes to death on his cross.

The last thing we need is some wannabe doctor who refuses to tell the truth. We need a real doctor who will give us the bad news so we can find the right treatment.

We need an accurate diagnosis. Otherwise we may never realize that our problem is so great that it demands our surrender. If we do not know how desperate things are, we may settle for something less than giving ourselves up at the foot of Jesus' cross and accepting the new life he offers. So in the end, an accurate diagnosis of our sin, while it is difficult to hear, is *good* news.

Fig leaves: Genesis 3:7

Isn't it amazing what we do in our shame? Adam and Eve recognize, in this new experience of sin, that they are naked. Why is this a problem? They've been naked all along and it hasn't been an issue. But now, when sin is loose in the world and in their relationship, they feel the need for self-protection. They feel the need to cover up their nakedness. They feel vulnerable, and they are.

We do exactly the same thing. We cover ourselves because we know that there are people in the world who will hurt us. Sometimes they hurt us because they are malicious and they are seeking to do us damage, but more often they are simply acting out of their own hurt and shame and we become incidental victims to the consequences of their sin. A teacher has had an argument with her husband before she leaves for work in the morning and her students get an extra helping of stern-and-demanding all day. Your boss dresses you down at work and you kick the dog on the way in the front door. It's almost a cliche.

But there's a deeper level to all this. First, notice that the fig leaves are an attempt to cover, to deny, our sin. But our nakedness is not our sin. We think our vulnerability is the problem and we try to "fix" it. So we build walls around our vulnerability. We promise ourselves we won't ever let anybody get close enough to hurt us in that particularly tender spot. We deny that tenderness even exists in us. If anyone or anything gets too close, we close off and wall up and walk away. Nothing to see here, folks. After a while we start to believe the lie that we don't feel, don't hurt, don't care, don't love.

It's all rooted in a hurt and vulnerability we'd just as soon deny. This is so often the story behind a married couple who say, "We don't love each other any more. There's no point in keeping up this sham." They head for divorce court thinking next time they'll get it right. But the root issue is the fear of hurt. They cover their unresolved vulnerability with fig leaves. The vulnerability and fear is still there and it destroys the second marriage, and the third.

The other part of this is that our disobedience to God hurts other people. We don't like looking in this mirror. Because our walls, our inner vows, our determination to avoid pain, are all disobedience to God who says, "Come to me and I will give you rest" (see Matthew 11:28-30) and "I am the Lord who heals you" (Exodus 15:26). We decide to cover and protect ourselves. And as we deal with our own wounds, everyone within range gets to share our pain. We don't like to admit it, but most of the wounds we inflict are involuntary. We don't want to cause pain. But the old cliche is true: "Hurt people hurt people."

Instinctively we know that our sin needs to be covered. That is true. But instead of going to God in repentance (which is very different from shame) we patch together leaves and make an ineffective suit that cuts us off from others and from God. We spend our time rearranging the leaves, patching the holes, and our attention is taken from a God-given focus outward.

That's what love is. Love is turning our God-given focus away from ourselves and onto another. Instead we turn inward, concerned about ourselves and our self-protection.

God wants to cover our sin AND protect us in our vulnerability, but these fig leaves are not his chosen instrument. He is wise enough to know that covering our sin, healing our hurt, and protecting us from sin's consequences will take much more than this breezy underwear we've woven.

So notice (leaping ahead in the story) what God does in Genesis 3:21. He makes effective clothing for Adam and Eve. What is required for them to be clothed in "garments of skins"? The shedding of blood. Something had to die to cover their sin. This animal that gave its life to clothe and protect Adam and Eve becomes a precursor, a foreshadowing. The implied bloodshed in Genesis 3:21 points toward Jesus who gave his life, shed his blood, so that our sin might be covered and we might be healed in the refuge of his love.

Walking in the garden: Genesis 3:8-11

So there are Adam and Eve, busily sewing up leafy garments
for themselves. Genesis 3:8 says that they heard the Lord God
walking in the garden in the cool of the day. Some translations
say "at the time of the evening breeze." The idea of wind is
there in the Hebrew language. So given the Hebrew play on
words where wind and breath and spirit are all the same
words, is this saying that the Spirit of God is blowing around
the garden? Or is it the pre-incarnate Christ in his physical
body walking around in the breezy garden? Or as Martin
Luther indicated, is it just that Adam heard the leaves rustling
and his guilty conscience drove him to hide?

Who knows? But if it's our story, you know as well as I do
that it's less important how God gets your attention than that
he does in fact get it. How does God get your attention? I've
noticed that he does this in a variety of ways.

I went through a season a few years ago in which God grabbed
me through songs on the radio. Seems like this is a more
frequent way for him to get hold of me when I'm jaded and
insensitive to his Spirit. He knows I need an audible voice, so
I'll turn the radio on and I'll hear someone singing words that
suddenly pierce my heart. One particular five hour road trip
about a year ago, I turned the radio on at three different times
for a total of about ten minutes. In that ten minutes I heard the
same song three times. Obvious much?

The first time I heard the song the words, "Why are you
striving?" jumped out at me. But I thought, "I'm not. I used to
be a perfectionist, but I got over it. I really don't struggle with
that any more." When I heard the song two more times, I
finally became convinced that God was talking through the
words of the song. And in that honest moment, God was able

to show me that I was indeed still in bondage to my striving for perfection. It was on that same road trip, after opening that door and beginning to understand this, that I turned the radio on one more time, asking God to please play something else. The next song that came on had the line, "Perfection is my enemy." He doesn't let go.

Other times God confronts me through the voice of someone I respect and care about. Frequently these people have no intention of confronting me with anything, they just comment on the truth they see. I do my best to surround myself with people who speak clearly and honestly about the truth. As they speak from the perspective of their own relationship with God, often the Spirit uses their words to confront me and I face the truth about myself.

Another way God often gets my attention is in solitude. One of the things I love about bowhunting is that it includes hours of sitting perfectly still in the woods. Granted, much of my time on a deer stand is given to thinking about deer, and that's okay. (I struggled through this one several years ago, when God made clear to me that he wasn't intimidated or bothered by my love for hunting and for the outdoors. He let me know in no uncertain terms that he created me with that love of losing myself in the wilderness.) I've cultivated many places of solitude in my life. On a deer stand, in a canoe, stalking through the woods or holding absolutely still. In those places, my mind has time to go quiet and listen.

Sometimes God gets my attention by thwarting and frustrating my plans. After my first book on the Exodus was published, I wanted to teach a class on that material. Three different times I planned for that class, and three different times doors closed and I was convinced that the time was wrong. So I gave up on the idea, convinced that God knew what he was doing. Then, when I didn't expect it, those doors opened and others on my team told me they thought it was the perfect time for me to teach a class on the Exodus, using my book. It turned out to be God's perfect timing.

How does God get your attention? And when he does, do you pay attention, or do you continue to hide? God not only comes walking through the garden, he calls out. He desperately wants a relationship with us. He goes looking. God is a missionary, coming where we are to seek us out. How will you respond when he calls?

Blame: Genesis 3:12-13

Do you notice how Adam and Eve invent blame? When God asks Adam, "Have you eaten from the tree I told you not to eat?" Adam immediately responds that it is the fault of this woman "whom you gave to be with me." In other words, it's her fault, and by the way, God, it's your fault.

So God plays along and turns, for the moment, to Eve. "What is this that you have done?" Eve's response is "The serpent deceived me." The serpent, God, that you created and allowed to be in the garden, so in the end it's your fault.

Both Adam and Eve (and you and me) are quick to blame God for things. We don't do it out loud, however, and we don't dwell on it. It lays under the surface and begins to create a wall of separation between us and God, a chasm of resentment that keeps us apart. In blaming God, we return to the basic sin we addressed earlier: We have chosen to know good from evil apart from knowing God. Then we turn our superior knowledge on God and judge him.

But perhaps the most amazing part of the story is that God never defends himself. He doesn't say, "No, it's not my fault, it was your choice" or "If you're going to be free to love me you have to have choices not to obey me as well" or any of the stock answers we give to defend God's honor. In fact, God seems quite unconcerned about his honor, at least in this context. And other places in the Bible he out and out says that if we're just going to have one God, he'll have to take responsibility at some point for the existence of evil. (See for example Isaiah 45:7).

This is a branch of theology called "theodicy." It is the question of how God can be righteous. We know that God is righteous, of course, but how is that possible when so many bad things happen? Frederick Buechner has put a fine point on the problem by laying out three statements:

1. God is all powerful.
2. God is all good.
3. Bad things happen.

Logically you can have any two of these statements but not all three. It doesn't work. If you say, for example, that humans have freedom of choice (which, by the way is a suspect statement if ever there was one), you have limited God's power (see number 1), so you can hold on to numbers 2 and 3. This is the solution Rabbi Harold Kushner adopts in his popular book, *Why Bad Things Happen to Good People*, by the way.

Or you can say God is sovereign, but we don't understand the reasons behind God's activity. Then like John Calvin we say that God consigns some to heaven and others to hell, and this is a mystery and above our pay grade so we should just accept it and not question too deeply. In this scenario we hold numbers 1 and 3 but we let number 2 slide a little bit, because how could a good God consign people to hell?

Or maybe we say (as is becoming increasingly popular these days as the pendulum swings) that "everything happens for a reason" and God is at work in all things to do good. Then nothing that happens is actually bad, so we can hold on to numbers 1 and 2, because we have let go of number 3.

You can't have it all three ways.

Trouble is, the Bible seems to make all three statements. Evil things happen. God is all powerful. God is all good.

People tried to pin Jesus down on the question of theodicy and he didn't do a very good job answering their questions. In Luke 13, they come to Jesus with a gruesome story about some Jews who had been killed by Pilate while they were in the act of offering sacrifices. The questioners were hoping for some sense of meaning, of justice, in this awful killing. But Jesus refuses to say the people deserved their fate. Instead, he says, this story offers you a great incentive to repent and turn away from your own sin, and turn to God in the face of such uncertainty. Then Jesus ups the ante a step. He tells a story about a tower in Jerusalem that collapsed at random, killing thirteen people. Life is uncertain and death is coming, he seems to say. So turn to God while you have a chance.

Is this helpful?

Probably not, if our goal is to understand what C.S. Lewis called "the problem of pain." But if the goal is that suffering should be the occasion that brings us closer to God, then Jesus' answer is exactly spot on helpful.

Adam and Eve miss their opportunity because they explicitly stop at blaming each other. Their blame for God is simply implied, just like ours usually is. If they would go a step further and rail at God, it would do them good. They could let their hurt bloom into anger. They could say something like, "This is such a comedy, God! How could you set this up this way? One tree right at the middle of the garden with the best fruit in the whole place, and then you say 'Do not eat of it'? This is stupid! Then to top it all off you allow the snake to come in here and lie to Eve! Is this fair? Does this make sense? NO." If they'd vent a little bit, they might come to the end of themselves and realize they need mercy, not fairness. They need love, not justice. They might come to a point of throwing themselves at God's feet and weeping for their sin and the brokenness they've brought upon themselves and on all creation.

The Psalms is (among other things) the Bible's book of railing at God. Oh, sure there are some beautiful worship passages as well, but the psalms are full of passages in which David and the Israelites lay out their laments before God. They blame God for evil, suffering, unfairness. Most of all they blame God for his silence. They rail at God for his failure to act, for his absence. It's scandalous to read some of these things. We can't say things like that. We know God is just and fair and righteous. We can't blame him for stuff.

But Jesus did.

"My God, my God, why have you forsaken me?" It's the first line of Psalm 22. Jesus cries out from the cross in abject misery with this line that leads into a poem of self-indulgent grief and pain. At the end of the psalm the poem turns again to faith and hope. That's nearly always the way of it. If we can be honest with God about our pain, sooner or later we will empty our reserves of anger and self-pity. We will come to the throne of God emptied of ourselves and ready to acknowledge him as Lord.

God isn't afraid of us blaming him. He simply wants us to come to him honestly, with what is truly going on inside us. That way our frustration can become a bridge between us, rather than a wall to keep us apart.

Messiah is coming

Genesis 3 contains what many biblical scholars believe is the first prophecy about the Messiah, Jesus, the One who would come and defeat the serpent. In his words of judgment on the snake, God says, "I will put enmity between you and the woman, between your seed and her seed. He shall bruise your head, and you shall bruise his heel." At one level you can read this and simply say, that means people don't like snakes. But at another level, it means much more.

The woman's seed, or offspring, in this case seems to point forward not to all humanity but to the one specific human sent by God to deal with the issue of sin that is now loose in the world. There is indeed enmity between Jesus and the snake, or Satan. They work at cross-purposes and are diametrically opposed to each other. Jesus sums this up in John 10. He uses the metaphor of a shepherd and his sheep. Jesus refers to the thief (not a far leap to read Satan into that) and says that the thief comes to steal, kill and destroy. Then he adds of himself, "I came that they might have life, and have it abundantly."

So the snake, Satan, is out to steal the life God gives. He wants to kill those whom God has made alive, to destroy all the abundance Jesus longs to create in us. Jesus comes to give us life, life abundant. These two are enemies.

How will it turn out? We've seen this enmity down through the ages. Cain and Abel, Isaac and Ishmael, Jacob and Esau, Joseph and his brothers, Moses and Pharaoh. Down through the ages enmity continues between people. Sometimes it's clear who is on the side of the serpent and who serves God; most of the time it seems the conflict plays into the serpent's desires and a God-given peace is all-too-elusive.

But God's words to the snake point to an ending. "You shall bruise his heel" sounds like a wound, but a non-lethal wound. "He shall crush your head," on the other hand, is a lethal wound for the serpent.

At the beginning of his movie *The Passion of the Christ*, Mel Gibson portrays Jesus in the garden of Gethsemane confronting Satan. Actually Satan keeps speaking to Jesus, and Jesus keeps speaking to his Father, which is pretty good insight. But while Jesus stands talking to the Father, Satan shifts forms and becomes a snake slithering around Jesus' feet. After he has prayed, "Not my will but thine be done," Jesus stomps on the head of the serpent. Not a bad picture of the relationship between the two. Certainly a nod to this verse.

I've been maintaining all along that this is *our* story. So?

How badly we need to hear this word, at this point! Genesis 3 has been sounding like such bad news. But this is the headline of good news to come.

When we are caught in sin, when we are blaming each other, when we are anticipating the heavy hammer of God's judgment falling on our heads, we hear this word. It is not a word of condemnation, but a word of hope. "He shall crush your head" sounds like we may someday be free from the bondage to sin, Satan, and death. Right now we live behind fig leaves, laying our shamed heads on our heavy hearts each night, but someday will come. Someday when the serpent is destroyed, the seed of the woman will conquer the powers of hell.

Theologians over the centuries have come up with a few classic explanations of exactly what happens for us at the cross when Jesus dies. These explanations are called "atonement theories." One of the three major atonement theories is called the "Christus Victor" theory. It says that at the cross, Christ won a victory over the powers of sin, death, and hell. Having won a battle against the powers that enslave us, Jesus set us free to enjoy the abundant life that he gives. We have been liberated, set free. Yes, we still live with old wounds. Yes, we have a long ways to go. But we no longer live in bondage to that scaly serpent and his lies. The son of the woman has set us free.

Let's put a personal point on this for just a moment. What is sin doing in your life right now? Where are you feeling the deadly bondage that holds you back from abundant life? Where are shame and blame having their way with you?

Can you hear this word spoken into your garden right now? In the face of that shame and bondage, can you hear God speaking to you? He is saying, Messiah shall come. He will crush the head of the serpent who is bringing death to you. He will heal the separation that has driven a wedge between you and God. He will take this shame to the cross, and he will die with your shame on his shoulders. You don't have to carry this any more.

What does that mean?

It means that whatever your shame looks like, you can bring it to the cross where Jesus defeated the powers of death and hell. You can bring it to him and lay it down. He doesn't deny it is real. He doesn't deny it is shameful. He is simply denying that it has to continue to keep you in slavery. He takes it onto himself and sets you free. He exchanges your shame for his abundant life. Get close to him and find out all that he wants to give you.

Judgment, part one: Genesis 3:13-19

God speaks three hard words after he confronts Adam and Eve with their sin. The hard word he speaks to the serpent, as we have said, points ahead to the eventual victory Jesus will win over Satan at the cross.

Sometimes these verses are called a "curse," or even "the curse." These words are a "curse" only in the loosest sense of the word. They are more consequence than curse. And this is the truth for us as well. God does not sit like Zeus in the heavens hurling thunderbolts at us. He's not waiting for us to fail so he can punish us.

Think of it differently. God has created the universe according to basic laws. They are good laws that help keep things functioning. One example of a good law God used in creating the universe is gravity. This basic principle holds the planets in our solar system together, keeps the moon in its orbit around the earth, keeps your feet on the ground and allows you to walk down the street. Gravity is a good thing. But if you step off a tall building, gravity is going to hurt you.

So it is with sin. God has placed basic laws in the universe. They are good laws that are used to make a good creation. The positive side of these laws make our best lives possible. For example, self-giving love is one of the best things in the universe. It makes the delight between a mother and child or husband and wife possible. It creates joy and security and all kinds of good things. But if you break that law, if you act selfishly, it's like stepping off a tall building. You're going to bear the consequences of your selfishness. Trust is going to be broken. Joy evaporates. Suspicion grows. It's as natural as falling off a tall building.

You can't break the law of gravity. The law of gravity breaks you. So it is with every God-given law. God is not hurling a curse-thunderbolt at his creation here. He's simply explaining how things are going to be now that sin is loose in the world.

To the snake, God says, "You've deceived my beloved; therefore I will put a plan in place to defeat you." In other words, you've set yourself against me, and so I will be against you.

A quick word about the balance of power between Satan and God. To put it plainly, there isn't one. There isn't a balance. The Bible does not describe a dualistic system in which the devil and God are equally balanced like some yin and yang. There's no question who is more powerful. The serpent isn't a patch on God, he doesn't hold any threat for God's goodness or God's plan. He's a fly in the ointment, to use a different metaphor. He can mar, but he cannot destroy.

To the man and the woman, God says, "Here is the consequence of your sin. This is what life will look like now that disobedience has infected your lives." His word to each of them is uniquely suited to the way he created them.

The woman is wired to focus on relationships. No matter what tasks she is doing, the woman is relationally-rooted. Even the tasks she chooses, more often than not, are important because she has a relationship with the people on the other end of the tasks. Whether she's doing laundry or making phone calls or going to work, she's thinking about the relationships involved. It's part of how she's created in God's image. So where does the woman experience the consequences of disobedience? Most painfully, in her relationships.

First God says she will experience pain in childbirth, and then it seems like the same idea is repeated. We call this common

Hebrew way of saying things "parallelism." Parallelism is a way of speaking or writing in which an idea is stated, then restated slightly differently. We see this very commonly in the Psalms. "The earth is the Lord's, and everything in it / the world, and all who live in it" (see Psalm 24). If the two ideas are identical, this structure is a way of lifting up the idea and showing its importance. But often, the second statement is slightly different, and the parallel structure is a way to say two different but closely related things. That's what is going on here with the woman. Here's how the English Standard Version (ESV) puts God's word to the woman:

> I will surely multiply your pain in childbearing;
> in pain you shall bring forth children.
> Your desire shall be for your husband,
> and he shall rule over you.

Do you notice that in the second line, God refers to bringing forth children? Not just childbirth, but the process of parenting. Oh, wait a minute... if that's what God is saying, it makes sense, doesn't it? Can you imagine how much less painful it would be to raise children in a world without sin? No rebellion, though a child would still struggle to learn independence. No selfishness. Instead we'd all be able to care for each other's needs, and our own, without fear. But in a sinful world, we struggle with all kinds of wants and desires and fears based on the fact that we know we're going to get hurt, and hurt badly.

Children are the second most intimate human relationship in the woman's life. Now God turns to the most intimate, to her relationship with her husband. Because sin is loose in the world, God says, the woman will have an inordinate desire for her husband. It's not that a woman wanting her husband is bad. Of course not. But because of sin, and the fear that goes hand in hand with sin, the woman focuses a lot of her hopes, fears, worries, and needs on that one man in her life. She desires him not for his sake, but for her own. She wants him to meet her needs in a way that insulates her from risk and fear and uncertainty. This desire grows beyond appropriate, godly partnership until she is willing to engineer the relationship to make sure it goes right. Though it's not what she wants, in the face of her fear she may decide to manipulate and control him to protect herself and bring about what she knows is the right outcome. Her desire is for her husband to lead her in the way she wants to go.

Something new enters into the marriage relationship at this point. It's a dynamic that has not been present before: the husband rules over the wife. In her fear she looks to him for protection, and that sets up an ungodly power balance. But then in response to manipulation he strikes back with power and a "because I said so" dominance. The man rules in lots of ways. Maybe through physical aggression and violence; maybe through passivity and passive-aggressive controlling behaviors. Maybe he controls her by abdicating his rightful place and staying at a distance emotionally and / or spiritually. When his wife begs him to get involved, he feels his power. Maybe he holds the financial purse-strings and controls the family that way. But this element of male dominance was not present prior to Adam and Eve disobeying God. It is not written into the created order. It's not God's intention. It is the result of sin. And the woman is trapped between her sin-tainted desire for her husband and his sinful controlling response.

God created this woman to be relational. She is designed to be connected to everyone around her. So it is in this area, the very best part of her, that she experiences the result of sin.

Next section we'll look at God's word to the man.

Judgment, part two

So what about God's word to the man?

> And to Adam he said,
> "Since you listened to your wife and ate
> from the tree whose fruit I commanded
> you not to eat, the ground is cursed
> because of you.
>   All your life you will struggle to
> scratch a living from it.
> It will grow thorns and thistles for you,
>   though you will eat of its grains.
> By the sweat of your brow
>   will you have food to eat
> until you return to the ground
>   from which you were made.
> For you were made from dust,
>   and to dust you will return."
> (Genesis 3:17-19)

The woman received the consequences of sin primarily in the area of relationships, in the area of her greatest strength, in the area in which she most reflects the image of God. The man receives the consequences of sin most deeply in his work. Adam was a farmer, a gardener. He had been given the task of tilling and keeping the garden. He was a namer and a caretaker, a planter and tender. He was made by God in God's own image; just as God worked to create, Adam works to tend and maintain. It's what he does.

Ask a man who he is, and most often he'll answer by telling you what he does. Men identify ourselves by our work. I'm a teacher. I'm a pastor. I'm a farmer, a plumber, a carpenter. I supervise a crew. I design buildings. I own a store. I run a restaurant.

In this identity we find our greatest satisfactions. Bob Buford has written about the shift men need to make after midlife, turning their focus from success to significance. Usually this transition involves a refocusing, a change in how we value our work, rather than a decision to toss work out of the picture. How many men retire and then take on a part time (or even full-time) job doing something else? Those who try to stop working don't last long in retirement. We need something to do. Even if it's a volunteer position or a task like building bird feeders, work is desperately important to men. It helps to keep us vital and alive. Men are about tasks. It's how we are created. And this is not a bad thing, it's the image of God.

Problem is, we are sinners living in a sinful world. So our focus on tasks, our being enmeshed in our work, gets distorted by sin. In the same way that the woman's focus on relationships is good, the man's focus on work is good. But sin gets into the mix and work becomes deadly.

Adam was a farmer, and when sin infected his work, the soil began to bring forth thorns and thistles. The frustration, the sense that our work is a meaningless "chasing after the wind" to quote the writer of Ecclesiastes, comes because our work is frustrated by sin. This is not some mysterious infection, it makes sense. If you supervise a crew as part of your work duties, take a blissful moment and imagine what it would be like if that crew was not a bunch of sinners. Think how delightful your supervision would be. If you are a plumber, think about how much easier your work would be if your clients, your suppliers, your coworkers, your mechanic, and all the rest were not sinners. No worries about being cheated. No worries about getting paid. No worries about people not valuing your labor.

See how it goes? Every job is frustrating and difficult because of the pervasiveness of sin infecting our work. Even those of us (and I count myself near the top of this list) who absolutely love our work find ourselves at times gnashing our teeth because of the fact that we have to deal with sinners. Worse yet, we ourselves are sinners. So we create all kinds of frustration for ourselves as well.

This reality, this pervasiveness of sin, leads to a sense of futility and meaninglessness at times. An old German man told me once that a German man's life looks like this:

> Work.
> Work.
> Work.
> Work.
> Retire.
> Build a house.
> Work.
> Die.

In that darkly humorous statement lies a sense of futility and frustration. How do I get off the hamster wheel? If I win the rat race, I'm still a rat. Right? It's just chasing after the wind. In the end, how much difference will I make? Late at night, staring at the ceiling, men ask themselves these questions.

Dust you are, and to dust you shall return. Your work, your effort, your earning, your significance, will come to dust. It will all return to the dust from which you came. And if we are wise enough to hear the words, we recognize that only at the cross do we find significance. The One who died there knows my name, and He is King of kings and Lord of lords for all eternity. All my works blow away on the wind, but Jesus remains. I will remain with him.

One more thing we need to address here. I've heard men joke about the opening lines of God's words to the man. "Because you have listened to the voice of your wife…" See? they say. I knew I shouldn't listen to her.

What's the problem with Adam listening to his wife? Trouble is this: He is passive in regard to what God has commanded, and he passively accepts Eve's error. This particular pattern is deadly and far-too-present in our world today. How many men sit through church because their wives want them to? So many men don't particularly care if their kids get a spiritual upbringing but it's important to their wives, so they go along with it. They are passive in regard to the things of God, and they passively accept what their wives ask of them. Not that their wives' desires are necessarily contrary to God's word, but if the man is obedient to her before he is obedient to God, how can he know what is right?

What the world so desperately needs today is men who are actively engaged in the things of God, actively weighing in and working hard on following what God has commanded them. We need men who are actively taking on spiritual leadership, spiritual authority, in submission to God and in order to love and serve their wives and children and communities.

God wants to redeem Adam's work. He wants to make it good and meaningful. But if Adam does the right work for the wrong reason, in primary submission to Eve rather than in primary submission to God, he will never experience the meaning, the fruitfulness, God desires for him.

Odds and ends: Genesis 3:20-24

In Genesis 3:20-24, God ties up a bunch of loose ends. These verses almost never get examined in any detail; we think the story is over and done. Sort of like how after the crisis, after the emergency, after the blowup or the breakdown, we don't often pay close attention to what happens in the mopping-up phase of things. But the reality is, those after-action moments can be some of the most critical pieces of setting a foundation for the future. So let's take a look at a few details:

1. God clothes them in animal skins. We've commented on this before, but it's worth revisiting. To give them leather outfits, God has to kill animals. Blood is shed to cover their sin and to protect them from its consequences. This again is a prefiguring of Jesus. The book of Leviticus tells us that without the shedding of blood there is no forgiveness, and we see it acted out right here at the beginning. What does this say about the nature of forgiveness? First, it is messy. Forgiveness, whether God's or ours, is not some neat and clean "oh-that's-alright" wiping the slate clean. Sin needs to be covered, not made as though it did not exist. Forgiveness is not denial. Whether here in Genesis or in the sacrificial system described in Leviticus or in Jesus' death on the cross, the biblical solution for sin is not to make it go away, but to cover it with blood. This could be a huge topic that would fill many books. But we'll move on.

2. Adam and Eve get kicked out of the garden, specifically to keep them from eating of the tree of life and living forever. It's tempting to see this as more judgment on God's part but this is really an action borne out of God's broken heart and his hopeful love for us. It's mercy. God is looking ahead to the cross, saying, "I'm going to cover this sin, provide a way for

sin to be dealt with on a permanent basis." The worst thing God can imagine here is that we should live forever in bondage to our broken, sinful selves. Truth is, the very best day you've ever had is still far, far, short of what God wants for you. That Very Good Day was still lived in the brokenness of sin, in the context of a broken creation. Someday God will fulfill what he began at the cross (see Romans 8 and 1 Corinthians 13) and we will live in the fullness of God's hope for us.

3. We are cut off from Eden. The text says an angel is stationed at the border of the garden with a flaming sword to prevent us from returning. Partly God does this to help us seek him. We are alienated from him by our sin. Being cut off from The Good Life helps us to seek God. It creates an uneasy frustration in us. It's a conviction that we were created for more than this. Ecclesiastes says God has set eternity in our hearts. In other words, he's placed an emptiness in us that yearns for him. We are cut off from him but still yearning to get back to him. As Augustine said, "We are restless, O Lord, until we find our rest in thee." This restlessness is part of God's grace, God's love for his creatures. We need that internal compass to draw us back to him.

4. The man is sent out with his vocation intact. He is sent out to work the ground, like God told him to do before sin came on the scene. The man and the woman are sent out together. In fact, it's almost a re-casting of the end of Genesis 1 where male and female look like two halves of a whole humanity or two sides of the human coin. God refers to them both by simply saying "the man." So both carry their vocations out of Eden. They are called by God to till the earth and keep it. The male focus in this vocation tends to be work oriented, the female focus in this vocation tends to be relationship oriented. But both keep their calling as they go out into a sin-broken world.

5. There are spiritual realities in this world that are out of our sight. We can't travel to the location of the Garden of Eden and see the impassable Cherubim guarding the way to the tree of life. Instead, in spiritual terms there are things going on we cannot see with our material eyes. We know that we are cut off from the life God intends for us, that this separation is rooted in God's love for us, and that the cherubim are beyond our sight. The goal is not somehow to get past this barrier and see the unseeable. Instead, we need to be asking, "What does God want for us now that we are broken by sin?" That's the question the rest of the Bible works to answer.

Names: Genesis 4:1-2

The Old Testament (and especially the first few chapters of Genesis) uses names in a very important way. People's names mean something. Occasionally there's a pun that sounds like something different than what you thought. Like when my friend was going to name his daughter Robin and I jokingly suggested Anna as a middle name. Just try it out loud.

Adam, for instance, is built on the Hebrew word "dam" which means dirt. So Adam is the one who comes from the dirt. And by the way, "adamah" in Hebrew means "blood" or "lifeblood." So there's this deep relationship in the name.

We do something similar in English. We are "human" and that comes from the same word-root as "humus," which means good soil for growing things. And incidentally, it's the same root as "humor," which is why so many of our jokes are "earthy." And because we come from the dirt and are a little "humorous" ourselves, we maybe should have a little "humility." Words can be fun.

Usually in the Bible, though, the names mean something, plain and simple. That's what we run into in Genesis 4:1-2. Adam and Eve have kids. Two boys. And their names mean something that becomes crucial to the story, but we don't speak Hebrew (most of us) so we don't get this part of things. "Cain" means "produced" or "production." So Eve says "With the help of the Lord I have produced a man." It is interesting to note that this is the first time (after the little fig leaf incident, which doesn't really count) that humans have produced anything. Tuck that in your hat for the moment.

By the way, let's take a short detour. Just for the record, there is no basis for the often-cited argument that sex is somehow linked to Adam and Eve's sin, that in the garden prior to the fall there was no sex. A God-given relationship that includes physical intimacy is laid out very clearly in Genesis 2:24-25. We get ashamed about our sexuality not because it's sinful, but because so often we indulge it outside what God intends. Within the boundaries God sets for sexual expression, it is an amazing, wonderful gift that was included in Adam and Eve's relationship from the start. Like everything else in creation, sex gets broken by sin, and shame creeps in.

What about the second son? Abel's name doesn't even get explained in the text. That's because in Hebrew, there's not even a joke being made. It's just a Hebrew word. To Hebrew speakers, it was obvious. "Abel" means "Empty." Adam and Eve had two boys, "Productive" and "Empty."

Now before you start to feel bad for Abel, think ahead. Better yet, read ahead. Read to the part where they both offer sacrifices to God. One of the oft-questioned mysteries in the Bible is why Cain's sacrifice isn't accepted. Is it possible that Cain is full of himself and what he has produced? Does Cain bring an offering to God out of his productivity and thinks God should be impressed? What about Abel, then? Is Abel's offering accepted because he comes empty of himself? That seems to be the implication of the names.

Try this. First, take a look at Psalm 51:17 and see what it says about the way we bring offerings to God. And check out Isaiah 57:15 and dozens of other verses that talk about God's attitude toward those who are contrite, beaten down, humbled. Or read the Beatitudes of Jesus in Matthew 5. It's also interesting to do a keyword search through the Bible on two words. First do the word "empty" and see how often God has to empty out something with which we have filled ourselves. Our wealth, our pride, our self-assurance, our security, our arrogance. God needs to empty us of all these things. Then look at the word "filled" and see what God wants to fill us with. Recognize that you can't be filled with the things of God if you're already full of yourself.

Sometimes the simplest lessons are the easiest to miss.

Offerings: Genesis 4:3-5

Genesis 4:3-5 tells us that both Cain and Abel brought offerings as sacrifices to God. For some reason Abel's offerings received God's favor, but Cain's did not.

From a historical point of view, this brings up lots of questions. How did they know to start offering sacrifices? How did each know whether his offering had received God's favor or not? What cultural context surrounded their offerings? Did God prefer lambs rather than grain?

None of those questions gets at the heart of this passage. There are clues here we often miss.

First, look at the specific wording about each brother's offering. Cain brought "some of the fruits of the soil as an offering to the Lord." Abel, on the other hand, brought "fat portions from some of the firstborn of his flock." Even in these two lines we begin to see a difference. Jesus taught that out of the overflow of our hearts we speak and act. So in the actions of Cain and Abel, we begin to see the nature of their hearts. Cain grabs a dipper and takes an average grain sample, as if he was going in to have the protein content measured. Abel, on the other hand, brings "fat portions." In other words, the best of the best, at least prior to our sedentary lifestyles and food pyramids. These fat portions Abel brings are selected from the firstborn of his flock. So not an average sample, but the very first, the very best.

What does this tell you about each one's heart? Abel gave an offering out of a sense of delight in honoring God. Cain maybe gave out of a sense of duty or perhaps even resentfully. (This attitude comes through in spades in the next few interactions he has with Abel and with God.) Out of the abundance of the heart, the mouth speaks, said Jesus.

So what's the point? I still don't believe it's a story about what happened back then. It's a story about me. And maybe about you.

What's your heart like when you give? Do you love to offer your best, your first, your "fat portions" to God? (Yes, I know, most of us wish God would simply make our fat portions disappear. That's not what I'm talking about, and you know it.) Or do you give out of a sense of have-to?

The trouble here is, our small-hearted giving bleeds over into other areas of our lives. If we are stingy in the face of God, we are also prone to be stingy and closed-fisted when it comes to relationships with others, and even with ourselves.

The deeper truth behind these brothers and their offerings is back to the truth of their names. As we said earlier, "Cain" means "productive" and "Abel" means "empty." When we see our treasures as something we've produced we will be tight fisted and small hearted. We believe we deserve some portion of the credit for what we have. But when we are empty of ourselves, when we realize all we have and all we are is a gift given to us so we might be a blessing to others, we can give generously.

Out of the abundance of the heart the mouth speaks. What's in your heart? What overflows into your hands and your mouth? What spirit do you present to the world? Is it a pride like Cain's, expecting that your gift is going to earn you some respect, or is it a joyful freedom like Abel's, giving yourself away without strings attached?

Get It Right: Genesis 4:6-7

> "Why are you so angry?" the LORD asked
> Cain. "Why do you look so dejected? You
> will be accepted if you do what is right. But
> if you refuse to do what is right, then watch
> out! Sin is crouching at the door, eager to
> control you. But you must subdue it and be
> its master."

What a hopeless word this is! If you do what is right, will you not be accepted? This is harsh and hard to hear, but it is so true.

First off, it's true when I want to shift the blame to someone else. I don't want to be held responsible for my bad attitude, my irresponsibility, my laziness. I want to believe that those are my negative reactions to other people's mistakes. My attitude is bad because people don't treat me well. I'm irresponsible because other people haven't held up their end of the bargain, so why should I try? I'm lazy because other people don't appreciate my work anyway. It's All Their Fault.

But God's word to Cain calls me on the carpet. "If you do what is right, will you not be accepted?" It's your call, brother. If you get it right, your righteousness will be recognized. By God, if not by other people.

So I'm held accountable for my shortcomings. It's my fault, not theirs. These are, after all, *my* shortcomings. And I hate that, but now I need to buckle down and get to work. So I start making to-do lists, planning my time usage, setting good priorities. And things get better in my life. But they don't get perfect. And when I see my shortcomings (still?!) I get frustrated. And God says to me, "Why are you downcast? If you do right, will you not be accepted?"

Then I resolve to work harder. To study more. To plan better. To manage even more effectively. And things get better. But they don't get perfect. So I get frustrated. And God says to me...

And I am broken, because I cannot do what is right. I can do some of it, but not all of it. I can be good, but not perfect. I fall short of the mark. Like Cain, I am an imperfect person.

So now I have an alternative. I can be broken, and my "self" (the essence of all that I try to preserve, all of me that I try to take pride in) leaks out and blows away on the wind. Or I can grab the duct tape and bind up my brokenness and try to keep it together. And try harder. And do more. And somehow make it work. And when it doesn't work, and I see others who seem to have been accepted by God when I fall short, I kill them.

Maybe not with a rock, but with my words. I gleefully spread malicious gossip about what they're really like. I take deep, hidden, evil joy in any misfortune that comes their way. I post scathing comments on their YouTube channel. These things make me feel vindicated, justified.

But the blood of the victims of my unjust attitude cries out to God.

The basic truth at the heart of knowing Jesus is this: we can build our lives on the barren rock of ourselves: our accomplishments, our abilities, our resources. Oswald Chambers writes that the definition of sin is "my claim to my right to myself."

Or we can die to ourselves and let our lives be based at the foot of the cross, on the stone of Golgatha, where Jesus bled out his innocent blood so that we might be accepted. Then whatever we have to offer is nothing at all. It is worthless in and of itself. But we offer it anyway in gratitude for what Jesus already did for us. We cannot be proud, but we are grateful. We are not resentful, we are joyful. We are not envious, we are delighted in the good God has produced in the life of our neighbor.

It's the difference between life and death.

It's not fair

We need to talk about something here. Reading these stories, from Genesis 3 onward, can break your heart. There's a deep sense of injustice in all this. Why are Adam and Eve, who were by definition innocent and unable to make an informed choice about sin, punished so severely when they disobey? Why did Abel suffer for Cain's failure? The stories will get worse as we go on, until sometimes reading the Bible is enough to make you throw your hands in the air and walk away. How can life be so unfair, especially to those who don't deserve to suffer?

Pay attention and you will find lots of people trying to address this issue with a variety of explanations of life, death, suffering, and all of it. Life is like a tapestry, one such idea goes, and we only see the backside of it. So what looks like a bunch of unrelated, ugly threads from our perspective, from God's perspective makes a beautiful weaving. What seem to us like unpleasant, ugly colors add life and texture and dimension to the picture. It's a beautiful thought. Or another metaphor that works in a similar way: life is like a symphony. The notes and chords that seem out of place to us add depth and beauty to the composition.

J.R.R. Tolkien, in the beginning of his masterwork *The Silmarillion*, tells a creation story of how Eru, the One, gave each of the Ainur (his version of angels) the gift of song, and then called them together to make a beautiful Music. But Melkor, the mightiest of the Ainur, had wandered long in the Void on his own and it came into his heart to fashion his song apart from the music Eru had placed in his heart. As he sang, others around him were drawn to shape their music according to his tones and it threw the Music into a great dischord. But

Eru raised up a counter-theme that took Melkor's harsh notes and drew them into an even greater melody. After this happened again, and again, Eru halted the song and told the Ainur that all creation would find that though they might rebel against the will of Eru, in the end they would find that all they did "only redounded to his glory."

If this life is a symphony, the themes are sometimes too bitter to be borne. The notes of this composition break our hearts and drive us to our knees, and rightly so. We must resist the temptation to call evil good. We dare not stand on the shoulder of the highway where EMT's and police officers pick up the pieces and talk about the way God sees beauty right here in this tragedy.

Even at the foot of the cross, where we know so much good was accomplished for us, we need to be careful about dressing up tragedy and making it look like something good. Yes, God does redeem evil and bring good out of it, but that doesn't change the fact that it is evil to begin with. We too often fall into the temptation of denying the reality of pain and suffering. We look too quickly toward the real or imagined purpose beyond it.

We take great hope in the idea that there is purpose in pain. It helps us to believe that at least from God's perspective, there is meaning in what seems to us so pointless and wrong. We long for a sense of security, a sense that in the end there is more than a nasty, brutish, short life that winds down with less eternal impact than sands running through an hourglass.

There are two edges to reality when we come up against these questions. The first, and hardest, is that it's too easy to make an idol of our own need in this regard. We are all too willing to make our desires for security paramount and view reality through this filter. So we manufacture meaning and recreate reality in a careful, closed system. We take the great mysteries (life, heaven, relationship) and recast them in ways that make sense to us. We imagine our loved ones becoming guardian angels over us, or we picture them in a heaven that looks a great deal like a beautiful childhood memory or an indulgent fantasy of self-gratification. So sports fans talk about that Great Baseball Game in the Sky. Or well-meaning, wounded Christians turn from worshiping God toward a cheap kind of ancestor worship in which they have conversations with departed loved ones instead of spending time in prayer. Neither of these pictures of an imaginary afterlife have any basis in a biblical faith. Of course there is grace here for the wounded spirit, and it is not helpful to chide grieving souls who need the comfort of a conversation with dad and a sense that even though he's gone, they can still connect with him at some level. But this is a practice of grief, not a belief rooted in the Bible.

The second edge is that, confronted with our childish imaginings about death and heaven, we sometimes abandon any sense of knowledge and we become, at least in practice, agnostic about the afterlife. For the reality is that the Bible is frustratingly silent on many aspects of what happens to us or our loved ones after death; but it does give us a great deal to hang onto. This biblical security is all rooted in the resurrection of Jesus. Where the Old Testament speaks hopefully about death, it does so looking forward to the resurrection of Jesus. The New Testament takes these shreds of hope and weaves them into a solid confidence that because Jesus is risen from the dead, we grieve with great hope. Our hope is not hope as the world gives, a sort of enthusiastic optimism (what my daughter calls the wishful thinking of the rabbit who, seeing the shadow of the hawk overhead, says, "It's just a cloud…") but Christ-centered hope. Christ-centered hope is the sure confidence that because Jesus is risen from death everything is changed and death is not the ultimate end of life.

I believe the Bible is silent about much of what happens after death so that we will not trust the process, but rather trust in Jesus. I don't know the future, but I know who holds the future.

So while it is unbiblical to imagine heaven as my ultimate self-indulgence, it is also unbiblical to say we cannot know anything about heaven. The Bible gives us a clear vision of being gathered together with the saints around the throne of God. There is communication, there is fellowship, there is joy and peace and music and celebration. We see Jesus face to face.

So we must not try to make Abel's death meaningful. Don't try to soften the blow of all the pain and suffering and tragedy in the biblical world, or in our own. Part of the tragedy of Cain and Abel is that this death, this suffering, this pain is unnecessary and pointless. This tragedy is reenacted in our world thousands of times a day in physical murders, and billions of times a day when I wound my neighbor and say, "I am NOT my brother's keeper."

It is meaningless precisely because it is contrary to God's desire. Abel's suffering is not part of the Grander Good. But in the face of Abel's meaningless death, in the face of unspeakable suffering, in the face of bitterness that drives us to despair, God intervenes. He does not undo evil, but promises that even in the midst of evil, even in the place of pointless suffering, even at the cross, he will be present to redeem and to heal. There is no tragedy so bleak that God cannot work in the midst of it. There is no suffering so dark that God is not present at the core of it.

In the face of death

After the death of Abel, we start to see creation disintegrating. Brokenness enters every human relationship. It's been happening since we disobeyed God in Genesis 3, but now we start to hear the cry of the human heart, alienated from God. Cain's lament sounds a lot like what my college profs used to call "existential angst." Cain is alienated from the ground, his brother, his place of origin, a settled life, God, himself, and other humans.

Existentialism is a philosophy which says basically that we are all alienated in this way. It is the ultimate individualism, in a sense, proclaiming that each of us is truly an island, each of us truly stands alone.

Death, which has been an unwelcome part of our story now since Genesis 3, is the final expression of this isolation. As the character of King Saul says at the beginning of the movie "King David," in death we are all forsaken.

Isn't this so much of what frightens us about death? We descend into this mystery alone, and though loved ones might stand around our bedside, they cannot accompany us. We are like children in a department store, playing peekaboo among the clothing racks, yet always checking to see if Mom or Dad is still close by. We want to dabble in isolation, we want to feel independent, but we don't want to be truly alone. Facing death is like that moment when the child looks around and no one is near. It's terrifying.

Instinctively, we shield our children from this as best we can. We don't talk about death, don't let them see death either in person or in the media. We speak of the dying in hushed tones and arrange babysitters during funerals so the kids don't have to attend. Notice that we are not carefully considering what is best for our children when we do this; we are simply acting out our own grown-up fears and trying to protect our kids from the nightmare that scares us.

Culturally we act out this fear of death by producing ever more bizarre, grotesque, and horrific visions of death. Horror movies or shoot-em-ups where bodies fly across the screen are common fare on our screens. I was driving my daughter and one of her friends home from school and the friend described in graphic detail a movie he'd seen the night before. On screen he'd watched literally hundreds of people die gruesome deaths. After ten minutes of vivid description, I asked him, "Have you ever been with someone in real life when they died?" He gave me a horrified look and murmured, "That would be freaky. No way."

Given our almost insurmountable fear about death, dying, and loss, it's no wonder that so many people wander our streets with hidden reservoirs of grief, terror and avoidance regarding anything related to mortality. It's no wonder that our children are shielded to the point where we create a phobia about death in them before they know what it is. They learn what we live.

The Bible says that death is the final enemy. What Jesus did, giving his own life and rising from death, flies in the face of our fears about dying and loss. Jesus' death on the cross does not minimize the reality of death; quite the opposite. Studying what Jesus went through on the cross leads us deeper than we ever wanted to go into the reality of death and dying. That's the point of the cross. Jesus enters into our deepest horror, goes fully into the most grisly death. Are we afraid of death because it seems senseless? Jesus' crucifixion is more senseless. Are we afraid of violence? Jesus dies at the hand of carefully, intentionally violent men. Do we fear prolonged suffering? The protracted torture of the cross was horrible.

Does the suffering and death of those who don't deserve to suffer and die offend us? Jesus was more innocent, more holy than any other. Yet he suffered terribly and died in horrible pain. Jesus enters fully into death in all its offensiveness, in all its horror.

This is the heart of the Christian gospel. Jesus, God in human flesh, actually suffered and died. By entering into our death, he conquered death. By rising from death, he demonstrates for us the promise of God who calls us into life beyond death. When we face our own death or the death of those we love, we can stand squarely without flinching, because we know Jesus has gone before us. We do not understand fully what this means, but we know that he has been here before us.

I sat on the riverbank with my daughter and her friends after the suicide of another of their group, and together they wept out the grief of those who were new to this experience of laying a loved one to rest. It's hard. My daughter knew me and my work as a pastor. She knew that I presided at many funerals and have laid a lot of my own loved ones into the earth. She turned to me and asked through her tears, "How do you do this, Dad? How do you do this over and over again?"

The question surprised me a little bit. I hadn't thought about it much. "I guess you get used to it, a little," I said haltingly. "Grieving gets easier. Not that it ever gets easy. But it gets to be familiar ground. You learn how to grieve." But then I paused, because I knew that wasn't the entire truth, nor the deepest. "But the heart of it is that I know Jesus. And he's been here before. He's been where I am, grieving for those he loves, but he's also gone into death itself. And he rose. He defeated death, and whatever happens, I know I can trust him to bring me, and those I love, out the other side of death."

So post-Easter, how do we deal with death, for ourselves and for our children?

First of all, we grieve. We do not lipstick a smiley face on death and try to make it okay. As Jesus' followers we know the horror and the pain of death. We do not minimize it or say it should be okay. It's not okay. It's wrong. It goes against God's heart for his beloved creation. So we weep, like Jesus wept at the tomb of his friend Lazarus in John 11. But as we grieve, and as we struggle with our own fears, we cling to Jesus. Amid all the flowers and weeping faces and clutter we place around death, we look for the face of Jesus, to look in his eyes and hear his voice. "Where are you in all this, Lord?" For we know he is there. He has been there, in death, and his promise is to meet us there. He does not simply come as the Comforter, though there is no greater comfort than the presence of Jesus. He meets us in the ambulance, at the hospital bed, by the graveside, next to the withering flowers at the weathered tombstone, as the Resurrection and the Life.

Second, in every area of life, we lead our children to know Jesus. We must do this in the midst of grief, fear, and death. So when my mother died without warning in 1994, or when my father died after a prolonged battle with cancer in 2000, or when my sister-in-law died after a medical procedure gone senselessly wrong in 2005, I was careful to sit with my children. I told them in words they could understand about this death, about how Grandma's body stopped working, about how cancer had taken over Grandpa's body, about how sometimes (not very often, but sometimes) accidents happen, even to people we love. I listened to my children's grief and to their fears. I let them see some of my own grief. I cried with them while they cried. I remembered and told stories and kept them close. And above all I let them know that Grandma, and Grandpa, and Arlene, are with Jesus, and he takes care of them, and we will see them again.

This is why it is much more difficult for the follower of Jesus to deal with the death of those who may not know Jesus themselves. But even then we can say, "We trust Jesus to take care of them," and we do. We don't know what the specifics are in eternity for every individual, but we know who holds eternity in the palm of his hands. He is trustworthy. When we know that our loved ones trust Jesus, we can proclaim their hope clearly. When we don't know, we proclaim Jesus and his faithfulness and his love.

But we need not, we must not, hide from death. This last enemy has been faced, and conquered. Jesus is risen, the victory won. And it is a real victory in the face of the ultimate enemy.

Brothers: Genesis 4:1-8

"Let's go out to the field." It's what Cain said to Abel to set the stage for murder.

The story of Cain and Abel is that much worse because of this treachery, this premeditation in the context of a relationship between brothers. Brothers and sisters are supposed to watch your back, defend your honor, and bear your burdens.

I am the third of six kids in my family. Stuck in the middle. As a younger brother, I imagine Abel's rush of excitement, no matter how old he was, when his big brother invited him to go along to the field. As an older brother, my stomach churns with the thought of betraying trust in this horrific way.

I think about what my siblings and I have been through. For example: my brothers and I bowhunt together. One night in the Colorado Rockies I was having trouble finding my way down a mountainside as night fell. I had stayed too long on stand watching for elk in a high meadow, and every trail I followed down brought me to the top of a 30-foot cliff. I knew if I couldn't get down, my brothers would be out in the middle of the night looking for me. Many times we have hunted bears together, and I can tell you there is great comfort in having brothers along on the trail of a wounded bear through thick brush in the middle of the night. We take care of each other.

It's what brothers and sisters do. We cook for each other and clean up after each other. We have worked together off and on most of our lives. We laugh together and tell stories and muse together to find the collective wisdom of where the deer are moving in the morning, or how best to work a herd of cows. We have sat in the pews together at worship services and at too many funerals. We have passed on hand-me-down clothing and favorite books.

How can Cain turn on Abel? God tells Cain before the murder, "Sin is crouching at your door." Cain turns his back on his bond with his brother and turns toward his own desires, fears, insecurities, and bitterness. This is what sin does. It turns us from God, from our brother, toward ourselves.

People sometimes ask how the Bible can teach that even babies are sinful. They're so cute, so adorable. But have you ever met anyone more self-centered than an infant? When we indulge our sin, we become more infantile, more childish. The sin that crouches at our door demands a pacifier. In Cain's case, pacifying his own selfishness meant killing his brother. It's a dark story, one of the darkest in the Bible, which is full of unpleasant stories.

But it is not primarily a story of murder. It is primarily a story about selfishness. And if we see it in that light, it hits much closer to home. How often have I turned toward my own self-indulgence rather than stepping out of my way for someone else? How often do I not see the needs of another person because I am so preoccupied with myself? I am not much different from Cain.

There is a Jewish story about a rabbi who asked his students if they could define at what point night gives way to day. One student replied, "When you can tell a cat from a fox?" No. Another said, "When it is light enough to tell a chicken from a duck." No. Finally the students ran out of ideas, and the rabbi stated, "It is daybreak when you look into the face of a man and recognize that he is your brother. For until that moment it is still night."

Surrendering our best

We often hear about "giving our best." Graduation speeches and corporate motivation seminars are laced with some form of the challenge to strive for excellence, to "give our best."

Sometimes giving our best has a whole different meaning in the life of the Jesus-follower. We see a foreshadowing of it in this story about Cain, Abel, and Seth.

Who?

Seth was the replacement son. He was the son God gave Adam and Eve to replace Abel, whom Cain killed. (See Genesis 4:25-26). The lineage of Jesus is traced through Seth, not through Cain or Abel. Seth becomes the carrier of God's promise, the reminder of God's presence, the agent by which God delivers the Messiah to the world. But Seth comes as the replacement for the one Adam and Eve had lost.

When I was about 20 years old, one of the character traits that I liked best about myself was that I was emotionally strong. By this I meant I was able to walk through any situation without getting emotionally entangled in it. I never wept. I could preach or speak in the most grueling emotional circumstances without choking up. I could walk into the most gruesome stories of abuse or tragedy without getting hurt myself. So, I thought, I was best able to help others because I could be strong for them.

Over the decades since then, God has grown me beyond that idea. He has crucified my best on the cross and destroyed it so that he might replace it with the very presence of Jesus himself, living in me.

So for example, God has worked for many years to tear down
and crucify the invulnerability that I thought was so good. He
has torn down my walls and allowed me to walk through
tragedies. Some of these were tragedies of my own and some
were the tragedies of others, where I came alongside as a guest
in their grief. These experiences tenderized my heart.

In one season when I worked as a full-time pastor, I spent a lot
of time and energy building a volunteer ministry team. In this
task I faced a crucial question. Would I maintain a
professional distance, by which I meant keeping my walls up
and maintaining my invulnerability? Or would I let these
people become friends, dear friends, who had access to my
heart? It was a tough question, and I wrestled with God for
months over it. I became convinced God was calling me to
open up my heart and let these people in. Always, I hasten to
add, making sure that appropriate boundaries are respected
and maintained.

To be honest, it was a frightening process. I thought my
invulnerability was the best thing about me. As God brought
what I thought was best about me to death on the cross, he
replaced that cool distance with a family affection for this
amazing team of people. In the process he drew the members
of this team into each other's lives as well. They became
friends, then family. For years they flowed in and out of each
other's homes. Kids ran from one living room to the next with
complete comfort. This group of people tended each other far
better than I ever could. Oh, and by the way, they became an
amazing team of ministry leaders who blessed many others
along the way.

During that season, difficulties came and went. One week we
began the week with a prayer service for Amy, one member of
this family. Amy was fighting cancer. That was Monday night.
After the service we went to her home and prayed over her

and her family. Holy moments. In the wee hours of Tuesday morning Amy met Jesus face to face. The rest of the week was a roller coaster of grief, leading up to her Friday funeral. This group of people who had become extended family to me and to each other broke my heart. I saw those I cared so much about in such pain. The invulnerability was certainly long gone as I wept with them and for them. And I wept for my own grief as well.

Several times in those days members of this team pulled me aside with some version of these thoughts: "Jeff, you know this is all your fault. If you hadn't pulled this group together and taught us to love each other, this wouldn't be nearly so difficult. Thank you. Thank you. You should be very proud."

As I write this, it's almost twenty years since that team first came together. Many of those families are still close. Some still work together in ministry. They still remember Amy. They still tend and care for each other in the wake of other tragedies. They still celebrate each other's joys.

I am not proud, for that would be like taking credit for something I didn't do. I had the privilege of watching the Holy Spirit build those relationships. I was as much in awe as anyone as I observed the bonds growing over those years. But I am so thankful that God took the best of me to the cross, to give me something better. He gave me Jesus and his vulnerability, his love, in place of my own invulnerability.

When God demands your best, give it to him. Let him nail it to the cross. Receive from him the brokenness, the emptiness, that feels so frightening. Let him grow you into the image of Jesus. What he will give you is so much better than what you would give yourself.

Running from God: Genesis 4:16

Genesis 4:16 could be a summary of what humanity has been doing throughout history. It says that Cain went away from the presence of the Lord.

Cain has received judgment for the sin of killing his brother. His violence, which grows out of his self-centeredness, has uprooted him from every life-giving relationship. He has become a wanderer on the earth. Yet God has marked him in some mysterious way to protect him from the violence of others. But now, Cain moves away from the presence of the Lord.

This is our natural tendency, our normal drift. We wander away like sheep (Isaiah 53:6). This is not a headlong rush toward self-destruction. But we graze a little here and a little there, drifting from one appealing bit of grass to another until we are separated from the Shepherd and wandering dangerously close to the edge of the precipice. When things are good and peaceful and things seem okay, we wander off like Cain, away from the presence of the Lord.

The next few verses tell us that Cain built a city, which he named for his son Enoch. This is not the Enoch we'll meet later who is descended from Seth, who "walked with God." That story comes in the next chapter. But Cain, true to his name (Cain means "productive," remember) is a builder, building up a city. He's busy with his efforts and his work.

I heard once at a leadership seminar a description of the difference between managers and leaders. If you have an expedition going through the jungle, managers are coordinating schedules, making sure the road gets built straight and level, scheduling shifts so that the workers get the maximum possible road-building done each day. Leaders are climbing the mountain miles ahead of the group, using binoculars and taking sightings and filling in the blank spaces on the map. The problem between the two occurs when the leader comes back and tells the group, "This is the wrong jungle!" The managers, at this point, are prone to say, "Don't tell us that. We're making good progress here!"

Cain is like a good manager. He's building stuff, getting a lot done. But he has moved away from the presence of the Lord. He's working in the wrong jungle.

How often do we miss the fact that we're working in the wrong jungle? The big questions of life are being answered in the wrong way, because we're focused on the fact that we're making good progress. This is the road to hell. It is not a road for axe-murderers and psychopaths; they already live in hell, to some extent. No, this is the road that Jesus described as a broad road with wide gates. It is the road so many of us travel, constantly monitoring our speed and gas mileage without ever thinking about our final destination.

It's a bit of a chilling thought, isn't it?

Walking with God: Genesis 5

It's always tempting to skip the lists. Peppered throughout the Bible are those lists of names, interminable lists of who begat who. Then there are other lists. Lists of sins, lists of sacrifices, lists of festivals, lists of laws. I once owned a Bible that put the lists in smaller print, as if to say "Nothing to see here, folks, just skip over this part…"

Most of the time that's okay. I would never encourage someone new to reading the Bible to plow through Leviticus, for instance. I would never encourage a newcomer to ponder the genealogy in Matthew 1 or the one here in Genesis 5. It's not the most important place to start reading.

Just for the record, it's generally not a good idea to start at Genesis and try to read the whole Bible. You can do it. But usually it's better to treat the Bible like a library, which it is. It would be foolish to go to the library and start at one end of the building and read every book on every shelf in order. If you're new to reading the Bible, start with one of the gospels (Matthew, Mark, Luke, or John). I'd recommend John for starters. Then read the other gospels. That way you get to know Jesus, who is of course the core of the whole book.

But later...

Later on, when you've gotten to know Jesus better, it's time to spread your wings. When you've read the stories in the Bible, when you know the characters and the names and the incidents in the Bible's overarching story, then it can be fun to dig through these lists. You can sift through a lot of gravel to find an occasional nugget of gold. It's in the genealogy in Matthew 1, for instance, that we learn that Jesus is descended from some women who highlight the sins of Israel's past. Tamar the unfairly shamed daughter-in-law of Judah (see Genesis 38). Rahab the prostitute from Jericho (see Joshua 2). "The wife of Uriah" more commonly known by her own name, Bathsheba (see 2 Samuel 11). These three strong women struggled to live in a male-dominated world that so often demeaned women. They are specifically highlighted in the genealogy of Jesus. By their presence in that list, they bring up some of the most troubling, most unpleasant aspects of Israel's history. Where's the gold in that? Well, isn't it comforting to know that God used these women in those disgraceful contexts to bring Jesus into this troubled world? And isn't it comforting to know that out of the disgraceful episodes of your life, God can bring good? (See Romans 8:28).

So what's in Genesis 5? Lots of really old people, for one thing. But the gem here comes late in the chapter, when Enoch "walked with God" and so didn't suffer a normal death. Enoch "was no more, for God took him." What does that mean? We don't know exactly. But out of this humdrum list of names like reading stones in a graveyard, we get this little glimpse of something better. Enoch walked with God.

In Jesus' own time, Enoch was something of a folk hero. They had written a book about him, the Book of Enoch, that made up all kinds of interesting tales about the derring-do of Enoch and the way that angels and demons fought in the heavens and what would come about in the end times. It was very popular reading in the time when Jesus walked the earth, though no one ever thought it a proper book to be included in the canon of Scripture. Many New Testament books are influenced by the Book of Enoch, however, and the little book of Jude even alludes to it. I suppose in that day it would have been equivalent to the *Left Behind* series of books today, or maybe *The Shack*. Interesting, thought provoking, but it will get you in trouble if you try to give it too much authority.

So what about Enoch? I keep coming back to that phrase, he walked with God. It takes me back to the garden where God walked with Adam and Eve. Enoch walked with God, and somehow his death wasn't like a normal death because of his relationship with God. The implication, I guess, is that God took Enoch bodily into heaven after 365 years. Sort of like God took Elijah bodily into heaven when he was too burned out to continue his ministry (see 2 Kings 2). I'm not too concerned about what happened to Enoch at the end of his earthly life, but the association between his non-death and his walk with God intrigues me. Because I've seen it. I've walked with people right up to the edge of death many, many times, and I know that there is usually a striking difference between the death of one of God's holy ones and one who has limped along on their own two feet all their lives, never trusting quite enough to be carried.

Those who intimately know what it is to be carried by Jesus' love and mercy know from experience how to trust Jesus. They face death with the assurance that here, too, Jesus will carry them as he has carried them many times before. Those who always have to stay on their feet tend to grasp at straws at the end of their lives. The dying person clings to the straws as they dissolve one at a time until finally they are left holding nothing, and they exit this life in a sort of helpless wishing for more to hold on to. When Jesus carries his beloved from this life, they look like they're getting away with something, slipping away like the delicious punch line in a joke that the rest of us, standing around the bed in tears, can't quite get yet. When the schemers and the limpers leave this life, they hang on to their last breath like it was their last nickel and they didn't want to go broke.

It's about trust, I think, and trust comes from walking with God. As we spend time in his presence, in his holiness, we begin to see life from a radically new perspective. We begin to find ourselves a little pathetic, a lot humorous, and unbelievably loved. We rediscover wonder. We begin to see ourselves and our surroundings as examples of a fearful and wonderful creation. The God who made all this is the one who, in Jesus, promises to meet me on the other side of death and carry me through.

Peggy taught me this. She was in her mid-40's and about to leave a husband and two children. Several days before her own death, we talked frankly about her relationship with God. She was having a great time planning her funeral, picking out songs and enjoying the opportunity to throw one last big party. She had worked through the anger and frustration and resignation and grief of leaving her beloved ones. She and I shared a few quiet moments while her family went for lunch one day. I asked if she had any concerns about her relationship with God, if she was at peace. She straightened up a bit and stared me sternly in the eye. "Pastor Jeff, I figure all I need to do is die, and Jesus will take care of everything else. If there's something else I need to know, you'd better tell me right now!" I laughed and said, no, Peggy, I think you've got it straight. More straight than anyone else I know. Peggy knew about trust.

Part of the truth of this is that when we walk with God, we can't choose the pathway. He gets to direct the route. We end up walking in a lot of places we might not choose to go. The valley of the shadow of death from Psalm 23, for example, or the deep waters of Psalm 69. Difficult places. But he leads us in green pastures and still waters as well, and he restores our soul, and we learn to know his voice and follow his lead.

Enoch walked with God. I like the sound of that.

Ripples on a pond

Throw a rock into the water on a still day. Watch the circles grow larger and larger. The impact of that one little splash spreads outward, changing everything around it.

Eve has a conversation with a snake and disobeys God. That's one tiny interaction. But then it expands out to impact her marriage, and Adam's vocation, and their living arrangements, and their children, and society as a whole...

Sin is insidious and it spreads like a bad cold. Sometimes you can watch the disease leap from one person to another; other times it seems like it's spreading on the wind.

In Genesis 6 sin makes a leap from humankind into the cosmos in general. What's this business about the "sons of God" lusting after and marrying human women? Various interpreters have had a field day with what is actually being talked about. Fiction writers from The Book of Enoch on down to fantasy writers in our own day have had a great time speculating about these "nephilim." Most of the speculation is entertaining, but from a wider biblical perspective a bit foolish.

The Bible doesn't make very clear what is happening here. What is clear is that there's a pretty significant boundary being crossed. When God created the universe in Genesis 1, there was a place for everything and everything in its place. Out of chaos (meaning, things go just anywhere, like my junk drawer), God created an orderly existence. But now sin has broken the boundaries and the result is a return to chaos. So here we see even the existence of orders of creation breaking down. Angelic beings have sexual relationships with humans, which was never part of God's intention.

Remember that we're not focused on what happened back then. It's so tempting to try to tease out what actually happened. But our question in this book is, what does this look like in my own world?

Nearly every ancient culture in the Mediterranean world had some story about the gods producing children with human women. The Greeks had the Titans; the Babylonians had Gilgamesh. The Egyptians believed Pharaoh to be a son of the gods. Each of these cultures looked to these cosmic cross-breeds for salvation. But the Bible is saying that this kind of half-breed divinity is not enough to save you. In fact, it results from a breakdown in the boundaries of creation. You need more than a half-divine warrior to rescue you from the powers of sin.

The irony is that like most counterfeits, this one is almost right. Because when God acted decisively to save this world, he engineered things so that he himself was born of a human woman. Jesus was not half divine, he was all divine. And all human. 100% of each. And rather than exalting himself as the mightiest warrior the world has ever seen, he humbled himself. His road to glory went through the cross.

So as sin expands farther and farther into the created world, breaking down relationships and throwing order into chaos, God is anticipating that someday soon he will move to create order, to heal the brokenness, to sacrifice himself for his beloved creation. In the next few verses of Genesis 6 we see the impact that sin's spreading has on God's heart. He is in agony over it, broken by the brokenness of his beloved.

The paradox of sin: Genesis 6:5-8

Read Genesis 6:5-8. Here we have a paradox. Sin is loose in the world like a hurricane; it sweeps over creation, breaking boundaries and reducing God's good order to anarchy and chaos. We, and the rest of creation, get tossed in this tempest. Yet in the midst of this terrible sin-storm, human beings are both victims and violators. We who are broken by sin are also the law-breakers. We are innocents who suffer the consequences of the power of sin; we are also moral agents who choose rebellion over and over again. It is a classic both-and.

Thus God can say that our wickedness became great upon the earth. Our wickedness, not the generalized sin of others. Thus in the face of the irresistible power of alcohol, the drunk confesses that he is responsible for his uncontrollable actions. The addict who has no choice repents of his destructive choices. And this is right and proper, because we are responsible in the midst of forces we cannot change. At the heart of our createdness we are made in the image of God, and so we are free agents. But in our free agency we are in bondage to sin and unable to free ourselves. In the German language, there's a difficult-to-translate word, "zerrissenheit." In English it means something like torn-apart-ness. It describes things that have been shredded. In the zerrissenheit of creation, we turn our backs on God, adding our small flow of putrid rebellion to the tidal wave careening down sin's sewer.

God diagnoses us accurately. Our wickedness has become great upon the earth. Every inclination of the thoughts of our hearts is only evil all the time. Some people object to this diagnosis, saying that humans are beautiful and wonderful and amazing. It is true. But we are infected with self-interest, and every thought, every action, every loving gesture, every altruistic breath is invested with our desire to make ourselves look good. You serve yourself. You love in order to be loved in return. You do your best in order to make your own world a better place because you will benefit. Many of us would die for the right cause. For our children or grandchildren. For freedom. For love.

Could you really give up your life if there was nothing in it for you? Probably not. Because sin turns every thought, every action, back in your own mind. Sin has its way and you don't know how *not* to calculate the return on your investment. You don't know how to give yourself away with no thought of return, no sense of satisfaction in the doing of a good deed.

Don't get hung up on this. You can't avoid it in this world. C.S. Lewis pointed out that one of the greatest things about heaven will be that we can live without selfishness, and what freedom that will be.

But don't try to tell God he's mistaken about your heart, either. Recognize the pollution in your motives. See the depth of the infection of sin in your soul. Understand the truth of what Calvin called "total depravity." It's not that everything you do is totally rotten like a fish dead on the beach after three steamy days in July. Rather it's that everything you do is infected with sin, like milk a few days past the expiration date. It just smells,and tastes a little off, and you can't make it good again no matter what you do.

The only way we can see this about ourselves is if we hold ourselves up to a very bright light. Most people think they're Pretty Good because they're examining themselves in dim light, in comparison to the faint glow of all the people around them. But the Bible holds us up to the bright holiness of God. As Matt Chandler has said, the holiness of God is frightening.

It's not that when you do bad, that offends God. We get that. The holiness of God is frightening because when you are at your best, offering the ultimate good you have to give, that still offends God.

When you recognize that you are depraved in the totality of your being, in every organ and every pore and every moment, then you need the cross of Jesus Christ. At that moment you are finally ready to bring everything to the cross. You can bring the good and the putrid, the noble and the diabolical to Jesus. At that moment of total frustration with your bondage to sin, you are ready to die to yourself.

We're poised at the beginning of the story of the flood. If we do not recognize our need, our infection, our disease, we will not see the point of this story. We need this flood. We need to die. We need to be drowned in the waters. This is our baptism. This is our crucifixion. This is our death. And oh, how we need it. Without this death there can be no resurrection. Our old body is beyond cure; the only answer is death and resurrection. The paradox comes full circle. When we finally let God put us to death, when the waters of this hurricane wash over us, when we drown in the baptismal flood like *Titanic* in the waters of the North Atlantic, we can *finally* be raised to new life.

Creation is broken.

We see this truth all around us. Creation is broken. Sometimes we believe in Progress: The best of our efforts create amazing capabilities, like the internal combustion engine. But to make your car work, we need oil. So there's an oil derrick in the Gulf of Mexico, pumping away because humans are amazing creative creatures. But something breaks, and now oil is pouring from a failed oil well into the teeming waters around it. Everyone from British Petroleum executives to shrimp boat deckhands to the President is suddenly scrambling to figure out how to deal with the brokenness of creation.

Not all of creation's broken state gets so much press, however. Here in Minnesota botanists are wringing their hands about a little bug called the Emerald Ash Borer. Pretty name for such a noxious critter. It is destroying trees and scientists don't know how to stop it.

Many years ago my family visited the Kenai Peninsula in southern Alaska. In the middle of the gorgeous scenery we saw mile after mile of spruce forest, dead and dreary, pointing barren tops like accusing fingers at the sky. They tell me a beetle was responsible.

We are tempted to romanticize the natural world. There's a temptation to believe that your version of the natural world is better than the alternative, is more beautiful, is somehow good and right. For decades there has been an argument raging about wolves. Hunting and poisoning and trapping decimated their populations across North America a century ago. Should we reintroduce them into the ecosystems around Yellowstone? Should we hunt them in northern Minnesota? Both sides of the debate have a vision of what the natural world should be.

Neither side can deal effectively with the objections of the other. The devil is in the details.

The Bible makes clear that sin's effects have spread far afield and now it is not only humanity that suffers from the effects of sin. Sin's impact is not even limited to that which we touch or that which we indirectly pollute. But creation's inherent goodness is somehow compromised by the presence of sin. Notice in Genesis 6 that when God decides to wipe sin from the scene, he not only has to take out the people; he has to eliminate "men and animals, creatures that move along the ground and birds of the air" in order to clean things up.

Lest you think I read too much into a simple Old Testament phrase, let's go look at Romans 8. Paul writes these fascinating words about the reality of the created world:

> For all creation is waiting eagerly for that
> future day when God will reveal who his
> children really are. Against its will, all creation
> was subjected to God's curse. But with eager
> hope, the creation looks forward to the day
> when it will join God's children in glorious
> freedom from death and decay. For we know
> that all creation has been groaning as in the
> pains of childbirth right up to the present time.

There's a lot to be said about this passage, but for the moment, see this: Humans in rebellion against God were the downfall of creation. Humans in submission to God through Jesus Christ will be its redemption. Whether this happens through the efforts of people who love and care for creation on this side of heaven, or whether part of our work after Jesus comes again will be the completion and tending of the "new heavens and the new earth," I don't know. Maybe a little bit of both.

The Buddhists have an intriguing idea. They talk about the interconnectedness of all things. One of their teachers has said that "all things inter-are." I have no intention of becoming a Buddhist, but I think that's part of what the Bible teaches us. As our sin infects all creation, so our nurture, our love can bring healing to it. Because we are connected in Jesus Christ, who is Lord of all creation, of water, earth, and sky, as the song goes.

So pick that spot you care most about and tend it. Make it beautiful. Let it become a signpost, a preview, of heaven. Why else would God give some people the gift of flower gardening? Without this understanding of creation and beauty and interconnectedness, it is such a pointless pursuit. But given the fact that God uses our sense of beauty to enhance and redeem a broken creation, gardeners should be held in high honor. If you doubt me, look again at the story of Jesus' resurrection in John 20. Is it possible that Mary mistakes Jesus for a gardener because the risen Lord had been digging in the garden and had dirt under his fingernails?

Sinfection: Genesis 6-9

The story of the flood is such a weird mix. And the way we treat it is even weirder. This is one of the first stories children learn, maybe because we think it's like going to the zoo. Noah takes two of every kind of animal, so we have pictures of bears and lions and zebras and giraffes and water buffalo and they're all lined up waiting to go on the big boat and the kids love it.

There is something charming about this story on the surface. You can almost see the newspaper headlines: "Local man rescues wildlife" or something. It warms your heart to think about it.

As long as you don't think too deep. Because under the patina of Noah rescuing a bunch of animals there is a nasty dark side to this story. Namely, the earth has become so violent, so corrupt, so sin-infected that God doesn't see a way out except to destroy it all and start over.

So how do you tell your kids that part of the story? Mostly we don't. Mostly we just tell the kids' version and let it go at that. In fact, across the whole Bible we often tell our kids, and ourselves, the children's version of the various stories. We never dig into the adult-level truths. That is why we find the Bible boring and unhelpful.

About the time your kids turn ten or twelve, as a parent you need to intentionally start letting them see what the world is like. This is tricky. If they haven't seen some of the dark underbelly of life by that time, you need to find ways to help them. Careful, now. This takes a delicate touch. You don't want to get them in too far over their heads. What about volunteering at a place like "Feed My Starving Children" or the Union Gospel Mission? Take them into an agency that is doing real things to help with real problems. Then talk about those issues at a level your kids can understand. Why are people homeless? Why don't people have enough food? What is a "refugee"? Why are there wars?

Lots of adults don't talk to kids about these things because they're not comfortable with the answers in their own minds. Guess what? Start this conversation and you might grow. Also, be careful not to give in to some half-baked political rhetoric when you go looking for answers. Don't blame homelessness on this or that political party. Don't blame wars on some bad guy over there. Be willing to see the darkness in each of us.

Noah pushes us to this growth. We would rather believe that sin is what everyone does, and God winks and smiles and goes back to managing the universe. But Noah forces us to see that sin has terrible consequences. God does not wink at sin; it breaks his heart. He has to wipe it clean, scrub it away, drown it. If he doesn't, God will see his beloved creation poisoned by sin. God has not set up the universe so that sin can coexist with his righteousness. His holiness overpowers sin and destroys it.

But even in the midst of this terrible realization that God is going to destroy the world, there is a word of hope, a possibility of redemption. Noah wasn't perfect. We'll see that clearly later in the story. But God chose Noah. Noah obeyed when God came up with a crazy plan to build a giant floating box. That's what "ark" means. So God used Noah and spared his life to repopulate the earth, to save the cute animals (and the not-so-cute ones).

No matter how sinfected your life is, God can wipe you clean, bring you through the flood, redeem you. This is the other truth that your child needs to hear and experience from you.

No matter how bad you are, God's love is deeper. God's love will work to clean the sin out of your life. He will preserve you and protect you and purify you because he loves you.

Looking for a relationship

Noah is an anomaly. He doesn't fit with the whole pattern. If God is out to destroy the earth, to wipe it clean of sin and evil, why save someone? Why not just start over with a robotic planet that does whatever it's told? Yet God spares Noah and uses him to save his family and lots of animals.

To answer this question, we have to look at God's love for his creation. God yearns not for perfection, but for relationship. So instead of destroying creation, he wipes it clean. But he saves Noah and an arkload of others.

There's an important lesson to learn here about how God works. God does not delight in destroying anyone or anything. God doesn't wait for you to mess up and then smack you. Rather, God is constantly on the lookout, even in the middle of brokenness and wrongdoing, for things he can use to bring about good.

Let's say you have a stubborn streak. Being stubborn is not good. But brought through God's redemptive processes, your stubbornness becomes a good thing. Maybe it becomes the root of your unwillingness to turn away from your faith. Maybe you become tenacious about things that actually matter.

Maybe it's your circumstances that are not good. You've been through some terribly hard things. Your suffering through difficult times opens a compassionate place in your heart. God uses this compassion to extend comfort and care to others who are suffering.

God is always looking for something to redeem. Noah
becomes the symbol of this. God is not seeking things in your
life that are perfect already. Rather, he's looking for things in
your life that give him raw material to work. Noah is not that
great on his own. We'll see this after the flood. But he's
willing to be obedient when God tells him to build an ark.

It's less about perfection and more about availability.

One of the devil's favorite tricks is that he gets us to believe
we have to make ourselves good enough for God. So we hold
ourselves back, trying to live better, be better, when all God
wants is really what we've just taken from him. God wants a
relationship. It is in the middle of the relationship that God
cleans us up and heals our hurts. Outside the relationship, we
are hopelessly on our own.

All of creation: Genesis 6:17-19

Two boys, clenched fists, swollen lip, tear stained glaring faces. Mom asks the inevitable question: "Who started it?"

The initiator bears responsibility. It takes two to fight, of course, but the one who started it...

God started it, and he's willing to take responsibility. Not just for a good creation. The goodness of creation includes freedom. Freedom is an incredible good. It allows for growth and maturation. But freedom also allows for disobedience. God is willing to take responsibility here too. He will purge his creation, wipe out the sin. But he will also make his covenant with Noah. God the covenant-maker creates something new: a covenant that preserves not only Noah's life, but also the lives of his wife and his sons and their wives and many, many other creatures. God creates a covenant that preserves life.

It is one thing to initiate punishment. That is usually simply a reaction to circumstances, reaction to other people's initiative. But God wipes creation clean AND initiates a life-giving covenant with Noah. Whenever we live in a relationship with God, this is God's agenda. He initiates his covenant. He defines the relationship so that not only is that person preserved, but God works through them to preserve life in their family, in their home, in their neighborhood. Each one who knows God is an outpost of God's love in a broken creation.

Here we see the poverty of western Christianity. God wants to work as he worked through Noah to create a covenant, and those who live in that covenant will become God's means to rescue creation. Instead, we took this amazing vision and said that living in covenant with God is a way for one (1) individual person to "get to heaven."

That idea, that knowing God is about us getting to heaven, is hard to find in the Bible. Pretty much impossible.

God is about rescuing and redeeming creation and we think it's about me getting saved. God's vision extends to our sons and daughters, cousins and uncles and nieces and dogs and the rabbits that live in the woods behind our house. God wants to save all of creation. Noah is a picture of how he does it. Where there is relationship with an individual, God works to save the neighborhood.

You see, now, how important it becomes, this choosing that God does? God chooses one person and a small corner of creation is drawn closer to him. God makes a covenant and a bit of creation is redeemed.

Are you living in covenant with God? He is calling you just as much as he was calling Noah. His agenda for you is nothing less. Build a mighty ark, a solid home, a loving family, a strong network of friends, a thriving business in which people, dogs, rabbits, trees, and flowers can be drawn into relationship with God. He wants to redeem all of creation through you, starting with the little corner where you are right now.

God started it with Noah. God started it in your life. His agenda, driven by his limitless love for his creation, is the same.

Closing the door: Genesis 7:16

The scene doesn't bear thinking about, but every movie portrayal I've ever seen of Noah's ark has included it. Imagine the preparation for the flood. Noah and his sons slave over plans and planks, hammers and hardware. Little by little they build this behemoth of a boat. The neighbors have tailgate parties, drinking and laughing at the crazy man who thinks it's going to rain. They think it's hilarious that Noah needs a ship to rescue all the animals and his family. Noah occasionally gets a fiery look in his eye and begins to rail at the neighbors, warning them of the wrath of God that will fall like a thunderstorm from the sky. They laugh louder.

The boat is finished, and the neighborhood becomes raucous with derision for Noah's foolishness. The only thing better than being a drunk is being a drunk with something worth laughing at. The neighbors mock and sneer. They laugh at Noah and his sons, who righteously begin to load all kinds of animals, two by two, onto the ark.

All this is based on the movies and our imagination. The Bible says very little about whether the neighbors laughed at Noah, aside from a couple obscure New Testament references.

In the movies, the scene changes as it begins to rain, and rain hard. Noah and his family and the animals are all shut up in the ark, and the neighbors suffer through torrents of rain. As the flooding starts in the low spots, they begin to become panicky. Finally they are beating on the sides of the ark in terror for their lives. But it is too late, too late...

There is one tiny biblical detail in the story that is worth mentioning here. It appears in Genesis 7:16, where the Bible tells us that "the Lord shut them in." It was God who shut the door on the ark. The weight of sealing that doorway, of closing off the way of escape to his neighbors, didn't rest on Noah's conscience. God did that.

Do you see what kindness this is to Noah? How terrible it must have been to think of his neighbors, even those who most deserved judgment, drowning in the flood waters. You can imagine Noah and his family shedding many tears over the consequences of wickedness, the judgment of God.

When God makes his covenant with you and declares you righteous, when he begins to work in your life to redeem those closest to you, there will be those around you who will resist his love. They may hear about your faith and sneer. Or they may go their silent way and reject the God who has found you. Depending on your style you may warn them, or try to persuade them, or pray for them, or ache for them. In some cases they will join you; in most they will continue to reject the God you love. But you need never shut them out of what God is doing in your life.

You don't close the door on them. You don't speak judgment on them. If that sentence needs to be pronounced, God will do it. This is God's grace to you. His grace is not only that your sins are forgiven, but that he spares you from having to pronounce judgment on those around you. You can live in love with God and let them see; you can speak a word of invitation to them when you are called to do so. But the final evaluation of their lives, the final closing of the door, is God's business.

We grieve when we see those who reject the love of God. For we know that their many sins became the bars of the cell that held them back from Jesus. And we know that all the while, God was yearning to unlock the door and release them from the cell of their own making. But in pride or in despair, they held the door fast shut.

When a life like this ends, we weep. We can be thankful that the consequences of a life squandered are not left to you and me. This is his mercy to us, even as others experience it as judgment. It is the same door. What matters is which side of the door you are on when the storm hits.

Destruction: Genesis 7:17-24

Genesis 7:17-24 gives a detailed description of the destruction caused by the flood. All living things that breathe on land were blotted out by the flood. Only Noah and those with him on the ark were saved.

If this is our story, what do we do with such a grim picture?

One of the basic ideas that grew out of the Reformation in the 1500's is the principle that we let scripture interpret scripture. If something in the Bible is confusing, let the rest of the Bible shed light on it.

The Bible helps us interpret this grim picture as our own. In 1 Peter 3 we read that the flood prefigures baptism; so just as Noah was saved through water, we also are saved through the waters of baptism. Peter clarifies that this saving happens not by the removal of dirt from the body. It's more of a drowning than a bath. Peter goes on to call it the pledge of a clear conscience toward God. Or as another translation puts it, "as an appeal to God for a good conscience." On what basis do we appeal to God for a good conscience, or pledge our clear consciences toward God? The phrase which immediately follows is the basis for the whole thing: "through the resurrection of Jesus Christ."

Genesis 7:21 says that "all flesh" died. Some translations say "all living things" but I like the ring of the older translations that say "all flesh." This is another phrase that points out the connection between the flood and baptism. In baptism, the "flesh" of the person baptized, their old sinful nature, is drowned. (See Romans 6:6 in context for more about this idea.)

Coming into a relationship with God through Jesus does not mean that I get a pat on the head and God says, "Good job! You're a pretty good person. You have it almost right; here, let me help you with the rest." Rather, the Bible tells us that when we come to God he puts us to death with Jesus, crucifies us like Jesus was crucified. Not one shred of me gets to remain alive. Even that which is best in me has to die. Why? Because only that which is dead can be raised to new life. If I cling to something of myself, if I cling to my sense of humor or my standing in the community or the fact that I'm a good driver, God cannot raise that part of me. Only when I surrender to Jesus, let him take me to the cross, can I experience resurrection.

This is terrifying. Don't you suppose Noah and his family and all those animals experienced some anxiety in the bowels of that giant wooden box? As they realized what was happening, they must have been terrified. But at that point, the ark was their best hope of being saved. So for us, the waters of baptism are a torrent that washes our life away, drowns us, destroys us. We cling to the cross in the midst of the flood and there God raises us to new life. Now what I am, the gifts God has given me, the talents and experiences of my life, can be brought to new life in Jesus. Now all these things can find their fullness because they are no longer mine, but God's. Now my life, too, can find its fulfillment because I am not my own. I have been bought with a price.

Before the rain started, all the people and creatures, as many as there were, were not a source of life for creation. They were operating in and of themselves, cut off from God's desires. If being alive means being in relationship with God, we have to measure things differently. When God finally washed the earth clean and saved Noah, his family, and a few animals, there was more life in the ark than there had been on the whole surface of the earth before.

It is the same in me. When I operate in my own strength, my
own wisdom, my own understanding, there is little life in me.
What life there is, is overshadowed and polluted by my sinful
nature. But when I surrender and let Jesus have my life, when
the cross becomes my cross, when I am united with his death,
then I become truly alive. This is the shape of the Christian
life. Surrender, death, and resurrection. My life is the flood in
miniature.

Endurance and purification

The Bible is very specific about the timeframes of the flood.

I'm always amazed when people say things are getting so bad these days. The Bible says the earth was "corrupt" and "filled with violence" in Genesis 6. Yet we somehow have the illusion that our days are worse than it's ever been. How is that possible?

The Bible tells us several times that the rains lasted 40 days and 40 nights. The ancient Hebrews used numbers to communicate symbolism. The Bible is full of significant numbers, from Genesis to Revelation. The number 40 is one that keeps popping up. It's here, with the flood. The Israelites wandered in the wilderness after the Exodus for 40 years. Jesus was tempted in the desert for 40 days before he started his ministry.

Without going into too much detail, the number 40 carried the idea of purification and testing. If God was doing something difficult in order to make his people clean, or to prepare them for something better, it usually came in 40s. So it's no surprise that the rains last 40 days and nights.

Then we read that the waters were on the earth 150 days. Some of you reading this are thinking about the hydrological cycle, wondering where all that water went. As tempting as it is, don't let yourself get focused on what happened back then. It's too easy to miss the point of the story.

As always, God is answering more important questions. He's telling you who he is and how he works. And he's explaining your life.

When God decides to clean you up, it's not always an easy
process. The things in your life that are designed to purify you
can be so difficult. An alcoholic who decides to enter
treatment faces a tough time. A person who decides to get
their finances in order after a season of self-indulgence will
feel the pain of self-discipline. Someone who gets serious
about losing a few pounds will struggle.

It's the same when God wants to clean you up and prepare you
for something better. The children's version has smiling Noah
and a bunch of happy animals entering the ark. But if you've
ever lived in a close-knit community, you can imagine the
challenges of being stuck for 150 days in a box floating on the
water with the manure building up.

It takes time to change habits. It takes time to learn discipline.
40 days is not a bad time frame if you want to make a serious
change in your life.

After that period of endurance, release comes slowly. Noah
sends out birds, and there's no sign of life yet. He and all the
others stay in the ark even after it comes to rest on the
mountains of Ararat. Bird after bird, until one finally brings
back an olive leaf. Still he waited, seven more days, and then
when he sent the dove out she didn't return. Finally it was
time for them to come out of the ark. Still Noah waited until
God commanded him to leave.

What's to learn?

Be patient when God has you in a time of endurance. Change
takes longer and will be harder than you expect. God has not
abandoned you. Look around and see that he has provided a
place of refuge, a place of deliverance. Even if it's cramped
and smells to high heaven. Endure in this season of
purification, and know that God is using this time to scrub
some things clean in your life. He's killing what has to die and

bringing about new life. Wait for him. When it's time, enter into the new life slowly. Don't rush to take hold of the new season until God opens the way for you. When it's time, he'll let you know.

When Noah leaves the ark, the first thing he does is worship. He builds an altar to the Lord. In that moment, God speaks a powerful word of promise. *Never again.* He disrupted the seasons, the rhythms of life to destroy all life. Never again.

Even if it feels like your life has been totally disrupted, know that God has not abandoned you. The good structures of earthly life are intact. Spring follows winter. Day follows night. Harvest follows planting. These basic rhythms are reminders that God is creating life in you as well. He is for you.

We live in a world that is polluted by sin. Violence should not come as a surprise. We grieve for the things we hear about. Occasionally God works a season of change, and it's usually difficult. But even in the middle of difficult times, God is faithful. Bind yourself to him. Look to him. Trust him. New life is coming.

Fear: Genesis 9:1-7

I was driving down the road and saw two crows hopping across the road. That was not unusual, but the fact that they hopped, stopped and pecked at something, then hopped again and pecked again, almost like they were after a moving target, was a little strange. Usually when I see crows on the highway they're tearing up some poor animal that is not moving anymore because it's been thoroughly pulverized under the wheels of dozens of cars. As I got closer I slowed down a little bit. A salamander was trying desperately to cross the road, and these two crows were trying to eat it before it got away. As I watched, the salamander made a mad dash (as much as half inch long legs can dash) the last three feet into the ditch, dodging and weaving to avoid sharp beaks the whole way. The crows finally gave up and flew away.

I thought then about God's words to Noah after the flood in Genesis 9:1-7. For the first time in this story, God pronounces a word that fear will be the normal state of things. It's a little hard for us to imagine, but Genesis seems to imply that before the flood, there were no predators, no eating of meat by any creature. It was like Isaiah's vision of the messianic age in Isaiah 11, where he describes the predators and the prey lying down together and the lion eating straw like the ox. "They will not hurt or destroy in all my holy mountain," Isaiah says. Whatever the reality of this is for the predators, it is our own predatory selfishness that first needs to be subject to the Messiah's rule. It is our own prey-like vulnerability that God desires to protect. So it seems that Genesis 1-8 assumes this kind of harmony, and life after the flood is radically different. Now predators will hunt, and prey will be eaten, and all animals will be afraid of humans. The crows were right to pursue that salamander. They were following the order God has placed in creation. They are scavengers, first, but also predators second.

Sometimes this natural order makes us intensely uncomfortable. We don't want to examine this predator-prey relationship too closely. On a grand scale, we recognize that without the wolves, the deer become overpopulated and begin to die of disease and starvation. But very few of us are comfortable watching a pack of wolves pull down and devour a fawn. I grew up watching Wild Kingdom where most of the time, at the end of the chase the film crew made sure that the predator went off in search of easier prey. But the reality in nature is that life usually ends brutally.

This becomes even more difficult for us when we become the predator. We've exterminated the wolves from most of the country. Now we keep the deer herds in check as millions of orange-clad hunters wander into the woods each November. Even here, with high-powered weapons killing at a distance, there is often enough gore to turn your stomach. There is a touch of sadness, of grief, in the cleanest and most humane killing of a beautiful animal. Yet not to kill the animal is in the long run far less humane. Very few animals in nature die of old age.

A little over a hundred years ago, conservationists with the best intentions cordoned off the Kaibab Plateau north of the Grand Canyon. They hunted down most of the predator populations and forbade hunting by humans. Their intention was that the Kaibab would become a paradise for mule deer. Sure enough, for three years the deer population grew and filled the area, as though God's words in Genesis 9:7 were being fulfilled. But two years after that, it was nearly impossible to find live deer on the Kaibab. Carcasses lay everywhere; trees and underbrush had been decimated, and disease and starvation had killed hundreds of thousands of deer. Overpopulation is far less humane than a stable predator-prey relationship.

What does this mean for us? We find ourselves in a world where life comes only at the expense of death. Veganism is no refuge from this cycle; resources being what they are, you eating your broccoli means that the ground cannot be used to provide food for another creature. While there may be sound reasons for people who choose a vegan lifestyle, the ethical concern not to cause the death of an animal is not a reasonable basis for this choice. There is no life without death.

The fact that life happens on the shoulders of death is a bit of natural law that leads us again to the cross. In the death of Jesus my life is made possible. Out of his sacrifice I am spared. By his blood I am healed. At some level I may wish it was not so, but my wishing doesn't change reality, any more than I can rescue the fawn from the teeth of the wolf pack. Jesus sees reality more clearly than I do, and knows I cannot live without his death. So he, the willing victim, goes to the cross for my sake, and out of his death I receive life. I cannot turn aside from this or avoid this reality. It is truth.

Jesus is not ashamed of this. He is not resentful about losing his life, or powerless to save himself. "No one takes my life from me," he said in John's gospel. "I lay it down of my own will, and I have power to take it up again." A change begins when Jesus goes to the cross. Jesus named this change "the kingdom of God." This kingdom is only a foreshadowing now, only a foretaste. But someday, in its fulfillment, we will begin to see what Isaiah meant when he described the scene in which the lion lies down with the lamb, the child plays above the adder's den, and death is finally conquered.

Cursing Canaan: Genesis 9:20-27

It's amazing how little we pay attention to what the Bible really says. Stories we tell about Noah's Ark most often portray Noah as a gentle man, caring for his neighbors, heartbroken for the evil around him. We picture him as a prayerful man in earnest conversation with God. The Bible doesn't show any of that. In fact, up to this point in the text we know next to nothing about Noah.

It was God who chose Noah, and the Bible says that "Noah found favor with God" (Genesis 5:8). It does go on to say he was blameless and walked with God; but hold on to that for a minute. Have you noticed how quiet Noah has been so far? In fact, we haven't heard him speak a word. All we've seen is Noah obeying God's specific commands (see Genesis 6:22 and 7:5, for example).

Now the flood is over. We see Noah freed from God's specific commands and having to figure things out for himself. What's the first thing he does after leaving the ark? He plants a vineyard, raises some grapes, makes wine, and gets himself passed-out drunk without a stitch on. (See Genesis 9:20-27) His son Ham sees him and jokes about it with his brothers, who respectfully cover dad up with a cloak. Noah wakes up, probably quite hungover, and the first words we hear him speak are a curse on Ham's son, whose name happens to be Canaan.

Is this the guy children learn about in Sunday School? I don't think so. This Noah is a bit of an embarrassment, drinking and cussing like a sailor. He's verbally abusive to his grandson, playing favorites among his children. This from the man who is blameless?

Maybe it's post traumatic stress. After all, Noah has been through a lot.

Two things this story accomplishes. First, it gives us fair warning that the flood God sent to purify the earth didn't finish the job. While we learned in the process that God takes sin seriously, we also learned that sin resides in the human heart, including Noah's. We'll need a better cure than water to make us clean. So this story points us forward to the cross, where God washes us clean inside and out with the blood of Jesus.

Second, it reassures me. Because too often, I find myself acting exactly like Noah. Me and God, we're tight, and we accomplish great things, and then I turn around and disappoint my wife, or I'm too harsh with my kids, or I'm lazy, or gluttonous, or selfish. Noah's sin doesn't change the fact that God used him to do an amazing thing that preserved life. But even after the flood, Noah is still a sinner. Me too.

God chooses Noah, even as God by grace chooses me. And you. God doesn't pick us for his team because we're the best players. Instead, he picks us because he loves us, even though we don't deserve his love. It's a gift, like it was for Noah. And the gift of God choosing you is intended to overflow through you and benefit all creation, like with Noah.

So don't get obsessed with your imperfections. They're real, and they're not something to be proud of. But God has a lot of experience working with imperfect people. If you're going to get obsessed with something, how about the amazing grace of a God who chooses you in spite of those imperfections, and then works in and through you to do his work?

There's a second side to this awkward story.

Noah's curse on his son Ham, and specifically on his grandson Canaan, has been much abused over the years. The Israelites saw this curse as a part of God's mandate that they should take over the land of Canaan. In later centuries they believed they were to destroy or rule over the Canaanites. They also had the specific command of God telling them to take possession of the land and God offered some other reasons for this conquest. Almost always in the Bible, there's more to the story.

But this curse was also used during America's history to justify whites ruling over slaves kidnapped from Africa. When Noah says that Ham's descendants should be slaves to his brothers, it seems to justify enslaving Africans (the "Hamitic" or descended-from-Ham peoples) to the middle eastern peoples (Shem's descendants) and the European peoples (Japheth's descendants). So when white Americans of European descent wanted to justify an economic system that kept them in power, they used this text to legitimize slavery.

Now, be careful here. The Bible recognizes slavery as a reality in the ancient world. Our political sensibilities see slavery as one of the Ultimate Evils, and we rightly reject any sense that one race is inferior to another. I'm not at all saying that the Bible justifies bigotry or racism.

What I am saying is that we who read the Bible seriously and want to live by its guidance have to be very, very careful. The main danger is that we are all too prone to justify our actions and our systems, and we can easily read the Bible in a way that makes our preconceptions and preferences seem like the Ultimate Good.

We have to learn to read the Bible for what it really says. It's way too easy to make the Bible say what I want it to say. It's hard but necessary to let the text read us, rather than us picking and choosing our way through the text. So when I run into something in the Bible that makes me uncomfortable, rather than simply dismissing it or ascribing it to primitive cultures and their ignorance, I need to investigate. Dig into what the Bible says in other places about this topic. Wrestle with it. See how it relates to other places in the Bible. Then comes the hard part. When the Bible contradicts my assumptions of the way things are, I need to ask myself: am I willing to submit to this word? Am I willing to let God's Word shape and form my assumptions?

God's Word is eternal and inspired. My interpretations of it are fallible and culture-bound. Will I let the Bible read me?

Take a step farther. Can we also see that the Bible reads our culture? What the Bible has to say might not only contradict my point of view, but it might also contradict and confront our shared perceptions of how things are. For example: The Ten Commandments includes a commandment, or two, depending on which version and how you number them, that prohibit coveting. You shall not covet your neighbor's house, nor his wife, nor his manservant, nor his maidservant, nor his ox, nor his ass, nor anything that is your neighbor's. But every day in my mailbox I receive vivid flyers advertising everything from lawn services to law offices, from new cars to new hairstyles. All this advertising has one specific goal. It is all designed to make me covet. Listen to the financial reports and you rapidly get the idea that our economy is built on covetousness. If I'm not coveting enough that I spend rather than save, our economy will sag. It's all my responsibility as a consumer.

What does the Bible have to say to a society whose cornerstone is covetousness? What might the Bible say to us collectively about our desire for material things?

This is only one example. Dig deeper and you'll find dozens of other areas where the Bible confronts our shared assumptions about reality and how the world works.

Part of the problem with those slave owners and their supporters in the mid-1800's in America was that they jumped from "the Bible acknowledges that slavery exists" to "the Bible supports my desire to keep slaves." They failed to see what the Bible said at a deeper level about their economic and social institutions.

For example, they failed to take into account the verses where Paul specifically says that when Jesus has his way, there is "no longer Jew nor Greek, slave nor free, male nor female." And they failed to read the powerful message of liberation in the story of Philemon in the New Testament. The words were there all along, but they failed to read how these words critiqued their social and economic structures.

It's easy for us to condemn them, but are we willing to do differently? Are we willing to let the Bible read us?

What have we learned?

We've been slowly (oh, so slowly) working our way through the first few chapters of Genesis. At first the going was almost painfully slow, because there was so much in each verse to be wrung out of the text. And that makes sense. You see, we have a view of reality that is different from God's view of reality. So when we start reading the Bible, it's going to take a lot of work, a lot of thinking, a lot of learning to see things differently. Eventually we start to see that our assumptions don't match up, and we learn to see things the way God sees them.

We learn to accept some difficult truths, like the following:

1. God is. Genesis never argues for this fact or proves it, it's just there. God exists. Deal with it.
2. God creates. This gives God rights and authority over creation. (Fun fact: This creation includes us. God has authority over us.)
3. Creation is both intricate and good. God says "it is good" many times about his creation.
4. We humans are in some sense the part of creation most reflective of God. There's lots of room to think and learn and grow into what it means to be "created in the image of God" but that's what we are.
5. We are created for relationships. We are created for relationship with God and also with each other, and with the rest of creation.
6. God provides for our needs (not always our wants) by positioning us within creation. God uses natural processes (like the growth of fruit trees) to provide for our needs.

7.   There is a tempter, one who entices us to depart from fellowship with God. He is sneaky and bad. For some reason God allows him a certain amount of freedom.

8.   Given half a chance, we will go our own way. We will make decisions that seem sensible to us but contradict God's direction.

9.   The consequences of this self-will are devastating. We lose fellowship with God. We become aware of our vulnerability and don't trust God to protect us. We strive to protect ourselves. We blame others for our issues. We hide from the truth, from other people, from reality, and from God. We experience brokenness in our relationships and in our work.

10. God covers our shame, but this covering requires sacrifice and bloodshed.

11. God's covering does not eliminate the problem of sin. Sin continues to multiply. In the next generation it gets worse. It leads to the belief that I can please God by my actions, by my productivity. When our willful productivity fails to please God and get us what we want, we lash out.

12. Murder begets murder.

13. External solutions, even to the extent of the destruction of creation, do not solve the problem of sin. It is an internal problem, and we can't simply be washed clean. No external discipline will free you from sin.

14. New beginnings take time. It's okay if a new season starts small in your life. Trust that God is doing good things.

In Genesis 3-11 we see a constantly widening pattern, like ripples expanding on a pond. The consequences of our rebellion expand and expand. This is not a theory like the idea of an expanding universe. It is observable fact. Pay attention the next time you lose your temper, and watch how that little thunderstorm in your heart blows up and affects the world around you. Or think about the last time you chose to be less than truthful about a habit, an activity, an indiscretion. Your secret lie has power that affects your heart, your surroundings, your relationships.

Now we're going to see this alienation spread not only between individuals, but between language groups. Sin is spreading. Where will it stop? Hang on. God has a plan. It's coming. Trust. Wait.

Babel: Genesis 11

I've heard so many experts offer their perspective on the tower of Babel. For some reason biblical scholars have a difficult time just letting the story be the story. So here are a few of the ideas I've heard:

1. The Israelites were in exile in Babylon after the destruction of Jerusalem in 586 b.c. when this story was written. The Tower of Babel story was a commentary on Babylonian society. The Israelites looked around at the ziggurats and the Babylonian religious establishment and wrote a story critiquing the arrogance of the Babylonians.

2. One prof I had years ago translated Genesis 11:4-5 slightly differently. Instead of a city and a tower, he claimed the Hebrew should be translated "a towering city." In his view, the story of the tower of Babel was written during the reign of Solomon, when Israelite culture was moving from an agrarian, rural culture to an urban, trading culture. The glories of Jerusalem led the people of Israel to a sense of pride and their security was based on their towering cities. The story was written to critique the Israelites' own arrogance.

3. Others claim that this story was written at a time when the Israelites were starting to interact more with other nations and cultures and the function of the story is purely mythological. That is, the story is designed to explain the existence of different languages and cultures.

And of course there are more.

It is dangerous to get too hung up on the origin of biblical stories. First of all, there's a temptation to make the story something that is dependent on its human origins and limited by their perspectives and insights. Second, this line of thought pushes us to focus on the details of the cultures in which the Bible was written without ever calling us back to hear God's word for ourselves and our own culture. Whatever the origin of this story, there are important messages in it for us.

First of all, see how sin has expanded its sway. Rather than just individuals behaving badly, we now have willful, corporate sin. "Let us build ourselves a city, and a tower with its top in the heavens, and let us make a name for ourselves." Here we see humans at our insecure worst. There's no sense of trust in God or dependence on God in this strategy. Instead, it all depends on us and what we do. Let US build... We have moved from individual sin to societal sin. Our structures are infected.

It is easy to see ourselves in this story. It's fine to trust God, but when it comes to my bank account, my retirement planning, my insurance, I'm on my own. It's our story.

Second, the tower is a direct assault on God. The goal of the tower is to reach heaven. We are constantly tempted to try to bring ourselves to God. Sunday School children in a previous generation were taught to sing, "We are climbing Jacob's ladder, soldiers of the cross." Of course the lyrics neglect the fact that Jacob never climbed the ladder; rather, angels were coming down the ladder to earth. The God we meet in Jesus is a God who comes to us. We cannot get ourselves to God. When we hold on to our moral standing, our pretty-goodness, our sense of our own ethics and integrity, we are simply trying to bring ourselves to God. I'm not against integrity, of course; but when we think we have accomplished something for God by behaving well, we're sadly mistaken.

Third, we see in this story the awesome wisdom of God. He didn't need to destroy the tower, and that wouldn't have accomplished much anyway. Instead, he changed their languages. He cut off their communication. Interesting that the breakdown of communication is actually one of the side effects of sin. It divides us. God simply let their sin have free reign so they could live with the alienation that was brought on by their arrogance. This took the form of different languages that divided them from one another.

This Old Testament story has its counterpoint in Acts chapter 2. On Pentecost, God gave Peter and the other disciples the gift of different languages. God did this not to alienate them from each other, but to communicate the good news of Jesus Christ to many diverse people in their heart language. The burden of languages, the result of the sin of the tower of Babel, is transformed and becomes the means by which God proclaims good news.

This is the God we serve. He takes what we experienced as evil, as punishment, and he transforms it into good. When my arrogance is broken and I am humbled, I feel awful. But if I let God work in my humility, it becomes a tremendous gift.

That's really what this story is about. The curse of varied languages and cultures that alienate people from each other will someday be transformed as we come together around the throne of God, where people "of every race and nation, every tribe and tongue" will join in praising the Lamb of God (see Revelation 4-5). This is God's power to transform.

What looks like evil in your life? What looks like the negative consequence of sin, yours or someone else's? Can you imagine God transforming it and making it into a gift?

Something is changing

Genesis 11 is another watershed of sorts. In the beginning of the chapter, we see that sin has spread throughout the world. Not only has it separated humans from God, husband from wife, brother from brother, humans from the natural world, it now separates one group of humans from another. Think of all the hurt that comes from "our group against your group" kinds of thinking. We get so far into our own rabbit holes that our bigoted thinking seems right to us. We can't imagine how those other people can be so mistaken. They must be evil.

That attitude is what we see in the aftermath of the tower of Babel. This group is alienated from that group, and soon the two are enemies. Sin has spread throughout the world at this point and has gained momentum that will not quit.

But God has a plan. In Genesis 11:27-31 it begins. Out of Ur of the Chaldees, just at the southern end of the Plain of Shinar where that tower of Babel incident occurred, lives a man named Terah.

Never heard of Terah? Not surprising. His name only occurs in those genealogies that we blip over when we read the Bible. But if you haven't done it yet, read what the Bible says about Terah in Genesis 11.

God is well aware that his beloved creation is broken by sin. He sees the ever-expanding power of sin growing outward, breaking everything in its path. He is not surprised by this. Many people have asked why God would allow the tree at the center of the garden of Eden. Did God know Adam and Eve would sin? This is the kind of question that focuses on "what happened back then." If we focus in this way we miss the richness and truth of applying these stories to ourselves.

What we know for certain is that we are caught up in a world infected by sin. But God started long ago and enacted a plan. He's playing the long game, setting things up to come into creation himself. In order to do that, he will create a new nation. He will give them a land and a history. God is willing to spend centuries to heal his beloved creation. Imagine that kind of love.

God planned a way to bring Abraham and Sarah to the land of Canaan. It begins with a family move. Maybe the economy was better in Haran. Maybe Terah had itchy feet and was tired of Ur and all those Chaldeans. Maybe he got publicly disgraced somehow and needed to leave town. Genesis also tells us that Terah's son Haran died in his presence. This heart-wrenching detail might be part of the reason Terah moves his family.

In any case, he moves with his family, including the memory of his dead son. We don't know if the city of Haran is named for Terah's son or if it had that name before. Maybe Terah renamed the settlement once he got there, or maybe the name was a sign from God that his family should settle there for a while. Doesn't matter. In the grand scheme of world history, this seems like a trivial detail. One family moves from one end of the Euphrates valley to the other. No big deal. But out of these small beginnings God has begun to address the problem of sin.

Don't despise the day of small beginnings. Don't think the circumstances of your life are random. God is at work. In the next chapter he will announce his plan.

God's strategy: Genesis 12

Genesis 12 gets way too little attention. This chapter marks the moment when God goes from dealing with creation as a whole to reaching within creation to choose a path that will lead to Jesus. He is still working to heal all of creation. But his strategy will be to create one people group, and out of that people group to send Jesus to redeem all his creation.

Or to put it another way, in the flood or in the tower of Babel, God was dealing with all people, all creation. When he chooses Abraham, God focuses his love in a different direction. Instead of trying to suppress sin, he chooses one representative of sinful humanity. Then God promises that from this chosen one he will create a new thing: a priesthood. God will create a priestly nation, a people (Israel, eventually) who stand in the gap for all creation.

We have the benefit of seeing the plan from our perspective, looking back at the historical events around Jesus' coming. We read Abraham's story through the filter of Jesus. And we know that eventually this new nation, Israel, will lead to the Messiah, Jesus, God-with-us. He will not only plead with God for all creation but will give his life as a sacrifice to redeem creation. In rising from the dead, Jesus will conquer death, which is the ultimate result of sin.

It starts with Abraham and Sarah (actually their names are Abram and Sarai when we first meet them) and their nephew Lot, the son of Abram's dead brother Haran.

God speaks to Abram. "Leave your native country, your relatives, and your father's family, and go to the land that I will show you. I will make you into a great nation. I will bless you and make you famous, and you will be a blessing to others. I will bless those who bless you and curse those who treat you with contempt. All the families on earth will be blessed through you." Here is God's plan, or at least the beginnings of his plan. Abram will become a great nation, a blessing, an opportunity for the world to be blessed. From this point forward, this strategy will lay the foundation for the rest of the Bible.

Genesis 12:4 is one of the most amazing verses in the Bible. "So Abram went..." John Ortberg has said that "obedience is the means by which we experience (not earn) grace." Abram is not chosen because he obeys God; rather, he is blessed because he believes God has chosen him and acts in obedience to God's choice.

What small step is God calling you to obey today? We often agonize about the big choices, wishing God would make himself clear in the major league decisions. Yet we overlook the tiny areas where God's will is so clear. Over the years I've learned that when I am obedient in small things, it opens the way for God to guide me in larger matters. Are you willing to be obedient in small things today?

Abraham somehow heard the voice of God, and he obeyed. He took his wife and his nephew and their household and moved to a new land, trusting God to show him the right place.

If you have a sense of God's nudge to you in the tiniest area, step out in obedience.

Have you ever tried to push a stalled car? It's almost impossible to change the direction of a stalled car when it's sitting still. But if you get a couple people to push, and one turns the steering wheel, you can turn that big chunk of metal.

If you're moving forward, it's a lot easier for God to change
your direction. Step out in the small things where you know he
is calling you to be obedient. Let him change your direction
bit by bit as you move forward.

Looking forward

Now we are off and running. The next chapters will follow Abraham as he navigates the geopolitical realities of Canaan around 2000 BC, give or take. For most of his life he will be a nomad. By the end of his life he owns one tiny field in the Promised Land. He bought it from a Hittite man to bury his wife Sarah when she died.

It can take a long time for God to fulfill his promises. Be patient.

Abraham will grow impatient. He will question and doubt whether God is going to fulfill his promises. His children and grandchildren will struggle with this business of being the chosen people. Eventually they will grow to be a great nation, but it will happen while they are living in a foreign land, in Egypt. And then they will be enslaved there.

Much later, God will rescue them. He will make his covenant with them and turn them into a nation. He will raise up kings and prophets for them. He will give them his written word.

God works through the centuries to create Hebrew language, culture, and religion. He is not only working among the Israelites (they won't be called "Jews" until much later) but he is also working through the empires around them.

Through the Greeks and Alexander the Great, God will give the Mediterranean world a common language. The Greeks will also provide a common set of philosophical ideas that help people understand each other.

Through the Romans who came after the Greeks, God will set up a system of transportation and laws. The legacy of both the Greeks and the Romans will be invaluable when it comes time for Jesus' followers to spread the news that he has come. In fact, there was a narrow window of time in the century surrounding Jesus' arrival when all the right conditions came together. During that narrow window of time, it was possible for the good news about Jesus to spread effectively. Roman structures, Greek philosophy and language, and Jewish monotheism came together in a unique way.

Paul sums all this up in the New Testament book of Galatians. He writes, "But when the right time came, God sent his Son…" (See Galatians 4.) When the right time came. Genesis 1-11 sets the stage and defines the problem. In Genesis 12, God tells us how he is going to move in history to deal with the problem of sin. He is going to redeem his beloved creation. The rest of the Bible is the story of God working to bring it all about.

It's a messy process. God is not ashamed to work in the mess. He will get his hands dirty through the centuries. When the fullness of time comes, his Son will be born among farm animals and worshiped by shepherds. Jesus will be rejected by the elites of his people. He will hang out with the dregs and have a reputation as a drunk and a sinner, though he will never sin. He will die in agony on a hill outside Jerusalem at the hands of Roman executioners. He will rise from the dead and be mistaken for a gardener by the first witness to his rising.

Do you hear what a word of hope this is? Wherever you are as you read this, you find yourself in the middle of a broken world. Sin is at work all around you, shattering good things and bringing you to death. Everything external to you is infected by sin: your job, neighborhood, relationships, bank accounts. Everything internal to you is infected by sin: your giftedness, your dreams, your secret hopes and your most intimate desires. You are in bondage to sin and unable to free yourself.

God is not afraid of the mess. Through history he has risked his reputation time and again to put his good plans into action. He is at work right now, right there in the mess of your own life. He is working in you and in those you love. He is working in your circumstances.

At the cross, God's plan came into sharp focus. In his death, Jesus defeated the powers of sin and death. In his resurrection, Jesus initiated a new creation.

Someday God will bring that new creation to fulfillment. In the meantime, he is at work in and through you. At the cross he has forgiven your every sin. He is healing and cleansing you. He is calling you to be a part of his plan as history moves forward.

He is writing your story.

Appendix: Biblical authority

We're going to tackle the mythology question head on. If this
is important to you, please bear with me. This is going to
require some careful definition of words, and some careful
thought about what we mean and what we're looking for.

This question of myth cuts right through the heart of
Christianity, especially in North America. The question is
about whether we should read the Bible "literally." When I
have taught about Genesis over the years, people often ask
something along these lines. This was a student's response
several years ago to one of my teachings:

> Do we not run into danger theologically when
> we claim that certain scriptures are myth? Is it
> not not wiser to assume that God's inspired
> Word is literal, except in such cases as the
> inspired author directly states that the intent is
> poetic, prophecy, or a parable?
>
> With that said, I must admit that I am finding
> far more in Genesis than simply history.
> Thanks again for sharing your thoughts and
> theology!

This is such an important question. Our determination to read
these early chapters of Genesis literally says more about us
than it does about the Bible.

It is difficult, if not impossible, to understand all the trends,
movements, and patterns of thought we have inherited when
we pick up a Bible. As readers in the 21st century we do not,
we cannot, come to the Bible without a boatload of
preconceptions and assumptions. It is important for us to

understand what assumptions we carry and make sure they're the ones we want to carry.

Our thinking is shaped by the fact that we have inherited Rationalism and Humanism. No one asked us if we wanted these things. We took them in at the same time we were learning to feed ourselves.

Humanism is a movement or philosophy that began to invade western thinking in the 1500's, especially under the guidance of Erasmus who was a contemporary of Martin Luther. Along with Erasmus stood many other university teachers and leaders throughout Europe in the 1500's and later. The basic teaching of Humanism is that "man is the measure of all things." In other words, rather than receive divine teachings from the church without questioning them, we should evaluate everything and decide what is true and what is not according to some human-based standard of Truth. We are not subject to a greater authority and bound to obey it; rather, the human is the ultimate Agent, the ultimate one who can change things.

Rationalism, the working partner of Humanism, teaches that the rational mind of the human being is able to make sense of the universe and that Truth and Fact should be determined by the scrutiny of the rational mind. So if you have a problem, approach it logically. Make a list of pros and cons. This is a rationalistic approach, and by and large it is a good one. But biblically speaking, a rational mind is only one gift of God in creating humans. Oh, and by the way, humans are created under his authority, in his image, and expected to obey his will. We have to treat the assumptions of Humanism and Rationalism with caution.

Building on the foundations of Rationalism and Humanism, the Enlightenment is a philosophical movement that swept western civilization in the 1700's. The Enlightenment, as the name implies, saw itself as a great age of human growth and progress. In fact, it did give birth to lots of positive developments. At the same time, the Enlightenment shapes our thinking and assumptions in radical ways.

People have been writing history for ages and ages, since at least the time of Homer, who wrote the history of the Trojan War in a little ditty we call the *Iliad*. History through the ages, as everyone knew all along, was written by the conquerors. In the process of writing history, part of the historian's task was to help the reader understand events. To interpret. To collect some events and not report others in order to help us make sense of the world.

So for example, history students in North America have usually been taught a great deal about the European Renaissance because we viewed ourselves as inheritors of Northern European culture. We have been taught (until recently) very little of the amazing cultures that came and went in sub-Saharan Africa over the past 2000 years, mostly because the writers of history felt we were little impacted by those cultures. We report some things and not others based on what we feel is important. Please understand, it is impossible not to do this. When we study history, we will always choose some events to focus on and ignore others. Always.

A few years ago, about 185 years, actually, a German named Leopold von Ranke wrote that the task of the historian is to portray things "wie es eigentlich gewesen ist." In English that translates to "the way it really happened." Most historians since that time have adopted von Ranke's philosophy with some subtlety and nuance, because historians know it's impossible not to do some interpretation along the way.

The way it has trickled down to the average person, however, is that we believe, because we are rationalistic children of the Enlightenment, that history should be "just the facts, ma'am." And by the way, we believe that news reporting should be unbiased (or at the very least, fair and balanced). Listen to the evening news for a while if you can stand it. You'll see that this is pretty nearly impossible. When you report things, you choose some facts to report and not others. You bring your own sense of priority and meaning to the reporting, whether you're telling the story of a traffic accident or the Thirty Years' War. It is simply unavoidable, and in reality it's not even desirable. Because what we're truly looking for as we hear those stories is *meaning*. We need to know what difference this makes. How is this event connected to me and to my world?

So we're looking for meaning, right? But we don't want to sacrifice truth to get meaning. We want both.

Now, what is the best way to find meaning? Is it to look at unfiltered literal facts?

Think about getting directions. If you needed directions from Cub Foods in Elk River, Minnesota to Burger King (about three blocks) I could give you directions a couple ways. The first option goes like this: Exit the Cub parking lot to the east, turn right; follow that road through the stop sign and down the hill to the stop light. Proceed straight through the light and take an immediate left past the bank. Turn left into the Burger King parking lot.

Easy, right? That is because I have excluded every shred of information that doesn't directly bear on the question you asked: How do I get from Cub to Burger King? Your question frames the meaning you're seeking.

The other way I could give directions (and some of you have received this kind of directions) is to share with you just the facts: Go out the Cub parking lot to the east, the video store across the way is closing down, I'm not sure if they're still selling out their old DVD's any more but I was thinking about seeing what they have in stock. On the southwest side, back behind you at this point, of Cub down below where Target used to be there's a fenced enclosure. I heard that about ten years ago there was a bear in Elk River that got trapped in that fenced area. Oh, and Target closed that store down, inconvenienced a lot of people who used to shop there, and moved to the big new Superstore in Otsego, right there south of Rockwoods. They've got a white chicken chili at Rockwoods that's to die for. Well, they used to have it. The last time I was there it wasn't on the menu any more.

What was it you wanted again?

Both sets of directions are based on facts. Difference is, one set of facts is filtered by a question of meaning. The other is totally factual but unfiltered.

Which set of directions is true? In one sense, both are true. Totally factual. But the first set is a correct answer to the question, "How do I get from Cub to BK?" The question gives a filter that provides meaningful framework to the facts.

So what question is the Bible trying to answer? How does that filter change what's included?

Do you see how important this is? We play this "filtering" game all the time. Murder mysteries use our natural filters to fool us. When you find out it was really the hired hand who killed poor Aunt Betty, a part of your brain screams at the unfairness of the whole thing. "Uncle Al would have to have seen him on the road between town and the farm if he had done it!" you think. So you turn back to page 34 and sure enough, you remember something you filtered out the first time around: As Uncle Al turned the corner at mile marker 29, "he saw a man in a jean jacket hunched against the cold November wind walking along the shoulder of the road. Something was vaguely familiar about the man's walk, but

Uncle Al dismissed the idea and drove home…" It was the hired hand walking back toward the farm to commit the crime, but you missed it at the time. You filtered it out.

Hold that thought and let's come at this from the other end.

What are we really saying when we ask if the Bible is "literally" true? Are we saying that when the Bible reports history, that it is reporting it "wie es eigentlich gewesen ist," or to say it another way, "the way it really happened"? If so, we are taking our post-Enlightenment idea about history and imposing it on the Bible from our perspective. We are, in effect, insisting that the Bible, written thousands of years ago in the wisdom of God, should submit to our filters and our assumptions that have grown up in the last couple hundred years.

Now for those of you who are worrying at this point that I'm going to throw out the historicity of the Bible, let me pause in mid-thought to let you know that I am not one of those who say Abraham and the Patriarchs never existed, that the Exodus never happened, or that David never ruled a unified kingdom. People who deny the historicity of these things are called "minimalists" when it comes to the Bible. To all those questions I choose to respond by siding *with* the historicity of the Bible. I am no minimalist. I see nothing in any of those stories that tells me the Bible is doing something other than telling me basically what happened, and then extrapolating meaning from a series of historical characters and events. Importantly, we can correlate those stories in the Bible with socio-political situations, geography, etc., that we know of the ancient Middle East. So I accept the basic historical truth of the Bible's events *when they seem intent on being taken as history*.

But I don't want to risk missing the Bible's point by assuming that something is history if it's not intended that way.

There are times it seems like the Bible is doing something other than telling me what happened. I've made that argument repeatedly regarding the creation stories in Genesis 1-11. The books of Job and Jonah are two other examples of places where the Bible seems less concerned about the historicity of the story and more interested in the meaning of it. It's like a political cartoon, if you will pardon a trivial parallel. Is the political cartoon true? If it wasn't, it wouldn't offend anyone. It is the pundit's truth that earns him enemies. But sometimes to tell the truth we use an illustration or a personification. Or a myth.

We don't like the term "myth" much. We think it denigrates facts. We believe facts are more powerful than mere myth. And many people use the word myth to mean something that is *not* true. Basically they use the word myth either to mean a flat out lie, or they use the word to mean a funny story that has nothing to do with the truth.

If we're talking about simplistic stories of how the goddess Athena created the first spider out of a little woman named Arachne because Athena was jealous, maybe that's true. Nobody, not even the ancient Greeks, worried about whether Arachne was a historical woman or not. They told the story to explain their world. But those stories are myths because they once had great power to tell a people, the ancient Greeks in this case, about their world.

The way we're using the word "myth" in regard to Genesis 1-12 is to say that these are stories that are powerful. They function to tell us who we are. They are less worried about historical fact than they are about meaning. Joseph Campbell has written a great deal about myth and its power. One of my favorite quotes from his writing is about the function of artists in our culture. He says that artists "mythologize life." In other words, by portraying what they do artists help us figure out what it all means.

What is the relationship between myth and truth? As we said, sometimes people use the word myth to mean a story that is untrue. That's not what we're doing here. In regard to Genesis 1-12, we're talking about myth the way Frederick Buechner defined it. He said that a myth is a story that is always true. It is worth quoting Buechner at some length here. This is from his book *Wishful Thinking*:

> The raw material of a myth, like the raw material of a dream, may be something that actually happened once. But myths, like dreams, do not tell us much about that kind of actuality. The creation of Adam and Eve, the Tower of Babel, Oedipus–they do not tell us primarily about events. They tell us about ourselves.

> In popular usage, a myth has come to mean a story that is not true. Historically speaking, that may well be so. Humanly speaking, a myth is a story that is always true.

Every ancient culture had myths. Modern cultures have myths, too. These are true statements. One of our myths is that education improves your life. Another is that America has the greatest workforce in the world. Another is that in 1969, a group of American astronauts walked on the moon. I call these stories myths because in the culture I'm a part of, these are tremendously powerful ideas. They are statements that are linked to the basic meaning that gives power to my culture.

Careful, now. Please understand that I am not saying that those three statements are untrue. Quite the opposite. I know, for example, that there are fringe people out there who believe the moon landings were faked. No. Historically speaking, in 1969 Neil Armstrong stepped off the ladder of the Eagle landing craft and onto the surface of the moon. It happened. But that story is much more than an event. It's a myth because it carries great power to tell us who we are and what we can do.

Each of those three statements about education, labor, and the Apollo missions are modern myths because they tell us who we are and what is most important. They give us meaning. Education is hugely important and worth the effort if you want to improve yourself. America has a long, complicated tradition of innovation and effort to achieve amazing goals. (Look into the way we ramped up to fight World War Two, for example.) And the "space race" of the 1960's culminated in that amazing scene of Neil Armstrong stepping off the ladder onto the moon's surface. It was a moment that gave people hope and joy.

Many of our best myths have been written into movies. Have you watched the movie Gladiator? It's pure myth. Not because it's about a Roman soldier, but because it is about us and how important it is for us to hold tight to family, strength, honor, and duty. It is a myth because when Marcus Aurelius whispers to Maximus that there was once a dream that was Rome, but it was so fragile… he could as easily be talking about the freedoms of America, at risk from self-seeking politicians and the unthinking mob. Ohhh. Ouch. That's getting a little close to home. Exactly. That's what myth does.

I understand that there is a long tradition within certain circles of Christianity that says the Bible's integrity rises and falls on our ability to affirm and defend its basic *literal* truth. According to this way of thinking, Genesis 1 has to be literal. If God didn't create the world in seven twenty-four hour days (including one day for rest), the Bible goes down the sewer. One camp in the Darwinist Wars of the last century claimed this ground and fought themselves nearly to the death over it.

Because as soon as they defined the ground, they realized that
their literalist camp was divided between young earth and old
earth creationists. There are huge divisions in the literalist
camp. And there are huge divisions in the Darwinist camp.
Personally, I think both of them are missing the point. If they
want to focus on what happened back then, God bless them.
But they're in danger of missing what God is trying to say to
us in Genesis. .

I sympathize with the creationists' concern. I feel the tension.
If the first few chapters of Genesis are mythology, then where
do we draw the line? We're on a slippery slope and pretty soon
Jesus didn't really rise from the dead, it's just an inspiring
story about spiritual new life conquering all the deadly things
in our lives. I totally reject this view. I sympathize with the
creationists because I want people to trust the Bible. Most of
the Bible is telling us what happened historically. But it's also
doing much more than that. If Jesus' resurrection is only a
nice story, then it has no power. (The Bible itself says this
clearly. See 1 Corinthians 15.) But if it's only an event that
factually happened but it never touches my life with its power,
then it's meaningless as well.

In the end the literalists' argument has huge holes in it. In fact
the argument boils down to "inerrancy." This is a difficult
term. It simply means "without error." Some folks use the
word "inerrancy" to mean simply that the Bible is trustworthy.
And it is.

But when you dig into the term, "inerrancy" is a leap of faith
which claims that the Bible (not God, but the Bible) is totally
without error. The literalists realize that there are a few trivial
errors. There are discrepancies in body counts in two biblical
accounts of the same battle, that sort of thing. They admit
those errors have crept into the text. So the only way one can
hold tight to this belief in inerrancy is by claiming that the
original manuscripts (which by the way we don't have and

probably will never have) were without error. What the inerrantists have done to the Bible is the same thing the Pharisees in Jesus' time did to the Law. They build a fence around it and add in a little extra territory to protect it from all the unwashed masses like you and me.

Two major problems with this set of arguments:

First, inerrancy says the Bible I have right now is not trustworthy. It is based at two-thousand-years' distance on trustworthy manuscripts. Only the original "autographs" (those original manuscripts) are totally without error according to a strict version of inerrancy. This version of inerrancy is often called "verbal inerrancy." You will find it in the statement of faith in some churches, when they say that the Bible "in the original autographs" is without error.

Second, verbal inerrancy totally neglects and rejects the role of the Holy Spirit in maintaining and transmitting the written Word of God with integrity down through the ages. If the Holy Spirit has not been overseeing the process of transmitting the Bible, then the autographs don't matter.

I believe the Bible you hold in your hands is trustworthy. There are excellent reasons to trust the Bible. Do a little research and you'll learn that the Bible is far more trustworthy than any other ancient manuscript. While I maintain the integrity and authority of the Bible against all challengers, I cannot in good conscience buy into the idea of verbal inerrancy. As I see it, inerrancy is about a rationalistic need for me to control the authority of the Bible through human means (i.e., an unprovable faith in perfect autographs). Instead I'm convinced that the Spirit works in transmitting and translating the Bible to guarantee its integrity and authority down through the centuries. In the past, because of denominational politics and decision-making, I have publicly put my job on the line, publicly argued and taught, and finally changed my own denominational affiliation over the issue of the authority of the Bible. I have no desire to undermine the Bible's claim on me or to minimize its authority over me.

A man-made doctrine of inerrancy is a problem precisely because it doesn't allow the Bible enough authority. If there's a discrepancy today I can simply claim that some error must have crept in since the time of the original writing. If the advocates of verbal inerrancy claim that the original author was inspired to create perfect autographs, then (so they say) the text has to be in some sense inspired even if it's a little decayed and distorted with the passage of time.

We started with one of my students asking a question. (Remember that?) That student posits that inspiration rests with the author, and that it is the author's responsibility to tell us that what we're reading is poetry, parable, etc. If we receive no such notice, we should simply assume that it's intended to be taken as factual history.

Problem is (in addition to the above argument that the inspiration of the text decays over time if only the author is inspired) that the text doesn't often tell us what's what. None of the psalms start out with a notice that says "Note: This is poetry. Don't take it literally." Jesus rarely identifies his stories as parables, though he does so a couple times. In fact, under this system, we should assume that Jesus' story in Luke 15 about a man who had two sons is factual history, because Jesus simply says by way of introduction, "There was a man who had two sons…" Most of the places where Jesus' stories are identified as parables, they are identified not by Jesus but by the writer of the gospel story. Matthew, Mark, and Luke (John doesn't record Jesus telling parables) were certainly inspired, but I think we'd agree that Jesus has greater authority than they do.

The other problem with this whole line of author-as-inspired way of thinking is that the Bible seems to talk about the text as inspired, even more so than the author. See 2 Timothy 3:16-17, or Hebrews 4:12-13, for example. Inspiration is a difficult thing to pin down. Partially, inspiration rests with faithful authors who are doing their best to write in obedience to God. More so, it rests in the text itself that has stood the test of time in a faithful community that over time begins to view this text as authoritative, as God's word.

Here's a thought experiment for you to consider. At the end of his letter to the Colossians, Paul tells the Christians in Colossae to read the letter he sent to Laodicaea, and to have the Laodicaeans read this letter as well. We don't have the letter Paul wrote to Laodicaea. What if next week, an archaeologist dug up a copy of Paul's letter to the Laodicaeans? Would that be considered part of the New Testament because Paul wrote it? Or would it be an intriguing historical tidbit, but not scripture because it hadn't been included under the guidance of the Holy Spirit and the public reading of the Christian community over time? If inspiration rests with the author, the letter would have to be included.

Taking the Bible literally (by which we usually mean, taking it as factual history) is in many cases a good thing. Once we get to the stories of Abraham, for example, and beyond, there are clear signs that the Bible is giving us a historical narrative, though it's not the kind of history we usually expect. Even when the Bible is giving us a narrative that is obviously historical, the text is always, always up to something more than simple history. These early chapters of Genesis, however, seem to be doing something quite different.

Okay, so enough of diatribes. One final thought. What do I mean by mythology? I used the example of the story about Athena mentioned above only because both that story from Greek mythology and the biblical creation accounts are stories designed to tell us the truth about who we are and where we come from. But I hold the Bible's "mythology" on a totally different plane as far as its inspiration, the method by which it was written, and the authority that resides in the story. The Bible is the story that reads me. I am not willing to let Genesis 1-11 be just about what has happened in the past, though it obviously has very deep roots there. These are stories included out of the deep, deep memory of the Hebrew people. Over time they used these stories, under the guidance of God's Spirit, to tell themselves, and by extension to tell us, who we are. I know many people are certain that Moses wrote the first five books of the Bible. And he might well have at least written large sections of them. Even for the most strident Moses-supporter, however, it's obvious that there are some sections of those first five books that Moses could not have written. His death and burial, for example. And the vast majority of scholars agree that these five books have a long, complex history that involves many authors and editors.

When I come to these stories, I come humbly, expecting to encounter the God who created me, who knows me better than I know myself. He cuts through all my pretense and philosophy and learning and ignorance and changes my heart. I learn about the Enlightenment and Humanism and Rationalism so I can better understand myself and the baggage I bring to reading the Bible. I pray before I read so that my arrogance and my ignorance might not get in the way of being shaped by God as I read his inspired word.

I dare not make these stories simply about the past, because my heart is exposed in these stories. I have a sense God wants to use them to strip my soul bare and exchange my heart of stone for a heart of flesh.

The question of what happened historically is not settled for me. I'm not willing to surrender all the shreds of history from Genesis 1-11. But I get frustrated when we make it all about what happened back then. We don't realize that this story is describing us, that we are Adam, that we are Eve. But that doesn't mean I don't think there could have been a literal garden of Eden or that Cain really did physically kill his brother Abel. I think there are some great questions to speculate about wrapped up in all that. Some of the classic questions that budding theologians discover in middle school grow out of these debates. Where did the dinosaurs fit into the Bible? Where did Cain's wife come from? Did Adam and Eve have belly buttons?

But if we focus on "what happened then" we miss the more immediate and pointed question of "what does this story tell me about me and my life?"

Biblical authority is not so much about how you talk about the Bible as it is about what you do with it. When your life gets complicated or difficult, where do you turn? Is the Bible even on that list? Or when things are smooth sailing and you have time to work on self improvement, does a discipline of reading the Bible even enter into your thoughts or actions? When you see disturbing things going on in the world, how do you interpret those difficult things? What stories, what concepts, what sources of information help you figure that situation out? Is the Bible stored up in your heart more and more so that as you confront things in your day to day life, you make sense of these things through what the Bible says?

All the preceding questions point toward your attitude toward the Bible's authority. If you read it and use it to make sense of your life, you probably have a pretty high respect for it.

Next question. What do you expect when you start reading the Bible? Do you expect to read a document that tells about ancient times? Do you expect a document that teaches moral lessons? Or do you expect to encounter God in a real, personal way when you start reading the Bible? At some level biblical authority has a great deal to do with whether you believe God is active and present in the text.

Now push comes to shove. When you think or believe or act in a certain way, and then you learn that the Bible seems to teach a different way of living, what do you do? Do you dismiss the Bible? Do you assume that the Bible is outmoded and ancient, that things have changed? Do you argue with the Bible and try to talk it out of its position? Do you start digging into the Bible to find out if this teaching is consistent throughout? Do you recognize that you might need to change to adapt yourself to what the Bible teaches?

This previous paragraph is probably the highest level of living with the Bible as authority over us. If the Bible has authority over me, then I must change when I find that my life is out of alignment with it. I fully recognize how hard this is, and how challenging it can be, especially in our culture, to accept this. And admittedly, there are some bizarre things in the Bible that sound so strange to our ears.

If you're new to spending much time with the Bible, don't evaluate your life according to books like Leviticus and Deuteronomy to start with. Instead, begin with New Testament books like John and 1 Corinthians that will be a little easier to relate to. Focus on the gospels and the New Testament. Focus on Jesus. Eventually Leviticus has some amazing lessons to teach, but do yourself a favor and don't start there. But if I believe the Bible is God's book, and that when I read it his Spirit speaks through the written words to me, then I'd better pay attention when the Bible contradicts me. I'd better be willing to dig into it and maybe even change my behavior.

At some level, the deepest contradiction to my own life that I find in the Bible is this: Over and over, the Bible calls me to change things I cannot change, to do things I seem unable to do, to love people I cannot love, to give myself away

unselfishly. And I find myself stingy, unloving, and unwilling
to change. So at some level the Bible contradicts me in ways
that frustrate me and bring me to a place where I cannot be
good enough. I come to the end of myself and I recognize that
I cannot meet the Bible's standard.

At this point, the Bible has an amazing thing to teach me: God
knew I couldn't do it. And he has already done all that needs
to be done. He came to earth in Jesus of Nazareth, taught
about love and God and the Bible and compassion and
behavior and pride and lots more. We couldn't stand it so we
killed him in the most gruesome way possible. But somehow,
in the mysterious ways of God, Jesus dying on the cross took
my imperfection, my falling short. Jesus died for what the
Bible calls my sin. In return, Jesus gives to me his godly
perfection, his intimate relationship with God the Father. Not
so that I can do these things myself, but now when God looks
at me he sees the perfection of Jesus. He treats me as if I had
done all these things perfectly in myself. He knows I fall short,
but he pours out his love and his acceptance and his grace and
his blessing on me as a freely given gift.

Perhaps the ultimate measure of the Bible's authority is when I
am willing to accept *all* that the Bible says about me and about
my world. All the details of sin and falling short and
imperfection and my behavior that turns God's stomach. Am I
willing to look in that difficult mirror and accept God's word
about me and those around me?

Then I can also accept God's other word about me: not a word
of judgment, but a word of grace, a word of mercy, a word of
love freely given at the cross and empty tomb of Jesus.

Acknowledgements

I cannot begin to list the teachers and mentors who have impacted my faith and writing. I was raised in a household of parents and siblings who loved Jesus and read his Word. Growing up in rural Minnesota in a tiny church, I saw the scriptures held in high authority and lived out in community. Bible college and seminary equipped me to think, teach, and write about the Bible. Living, leading, and teaching in a variety of Christian churches over the years sharpened my sense of these matters. Decades of working to pass these gifts along to others helped me discern what beliefs and practices about the Bible bear good fruit, and which ones are destructive and counterproductive.

At every step along the way, I've followed in the footsteps of others. I've walked shoulder to shoulder with people who have sharpened, challenged, and encouraged me. And I've had the privilege to pour into the lives of others across the world. I'm grateful to each and every one.

AI technology was used to generate ideas for the back cover promotional paragraphs, but not for any of the internal content of this book.

No man is an island, and that is certainly true of me. I'm so thankful for all the saints and every community that has poured into my life and made this book possible. Thank you.

Thanks especially to a team of beta readers who offered invaluable feedback in the final revisions. And to my wife Lisa who has been reading and discussing these texts with me for months. You're the best, babe.

Jeff Krogstad, Spring 2024